Lovelorn

16 CLASSIC ROMANCE COMIC MAGNETS

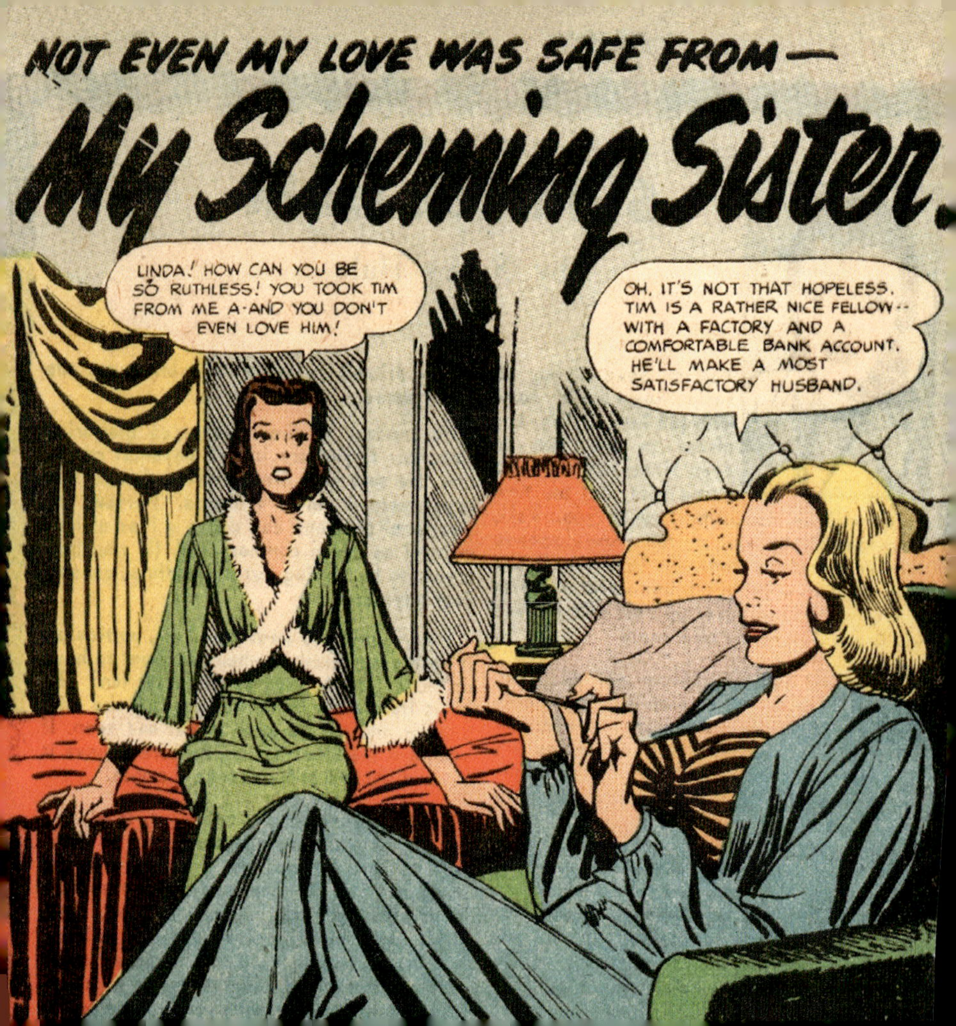
NOT EVEN MY LOVE WAS SAFE FROM—
My Scheming Sister.
LINDA! HOW CAN YOU BE SO RUTHLESS! YOU TOOK TIM FROM ME A-AND YOU DON'T EVEN LOVE HIM!
OH, IT'S NOT THAT HOPELESS. TIM IS A RATHER NICE FELLOW-- WITH A FACTORY AND A COMFORTABLE BANK ACCOUNT. HE'LL MAKE A MOST SATISFACTORY HUSBAND.

16 CLASSIC ROMANCE COMIC MAGNETS

• Tim Pilcher •

ILEX

♥ Lovelorn

First published in the UK, US, and Canada in 2012 by
I L E X
210 High Street
Lewes
East Sussex BN7 2NS
UK
www.ilex-press.com

Copyright © 2012 The Ilex Press Limited

Publisher: Alastair Campbell
Creative Director: James Hollywell
Managing Editor: Nick Jones
Senior Editor: Ellie Wilson
Commissioning Editor: Tim Pilcher
Art Director: Julie Weir

Any copy of this book issued by the publisher is sold subject to the condition that it shall not by way of trade or otherwise be lent, resold, hired out or otherwise circulated without the publisher's prior consent in any form of binding or cover other than that in which it is published and without a similar condition including these words being imposed on a subsequent purchaser.

British Library Cataloguing-in-Publication Data
A catalogue record for this book is available from the British Library.

ISBN: 978-1-908150-44-8

All rights reserved. No part of this publication may be reproduced or used in any form, or by any means - graphic, electronic or mechanical, including photocopying, recording or information storage-and-retrieval systems - without the prior permission of the publisher.

Printed and bound in China

Colour Origination by Ivy Press Reprographics

10 9 8 7 6 5 4 3 2 1

Contents

♡♡♡♡♡♡♡♡♡♡♡♡

♡ 6   A Brief History of American Romance Comics

♡ 16   The Magnets and the Stories Behind Them

A Brief History of American Romance Comics

It's hard to believe now, but shortly after World War II comic books were one of the biggest forms of mass media entertainment in America, selling millions of copies to adults and children across the country every month. During the war the patriotic efforts of superheroes bashing the hell out of Nazis and "Japs" in Europe and the South Pacific helped boost morale and entertained troops and civilians alike. But after the war the spandex-clad heroes seemed passé and outmoded and the genre was in decline.

Two of the greatest comic creators to emerge in the pre-war comics boom were Joe Simon and Jack Kirby—who created one of comics' most enduring superhero icons, Captain America. But the writer/artists could see the writing on the wall for their type of tale and started hunting around for new genres.

"I noticed there were so many adults, the officers and men, the people in the town, reading kids' comic books," recalled Simon, "I felt sure there should be an adult comic book." He looked around and settled on romance as the perfect genre as "it was about the only thing that hadn't been done."

Simon and Kirby developed a first-issue of *Young Romance*—along with Bill Draut and other artists—and Simon took his inspiration for the strips from the darker-toned confession magazines such as *True Story* and struck gold.

The first issue of *Young Romance*—cover-dated September-October, 1947—bore the tagline "Designed For The More ADULT Readers of Comics," hinting at perhaps more salacious content than the title actually contained. Regardless of the false advertising on the cover—something that would become an industry standard—the title sold an impressive 92% of its print run, and the third issue tripled the circulation to 1,000,000 copies! *Young Romance* switched from bimonthly to monthly and spawned the spin-off *Young Love*. These two were quickly followed by *Young Brides* and *In Love*.

Teen-Age Romances #34 (November, 1953)
Matt Baker

Asking for Trouble sees wanton, big city hussy Hilda destroy small town teenagers' lives with her lascivious parties and "bad-girl" attitude, only for her to discover the error of her ways and repent. It is a "true story."

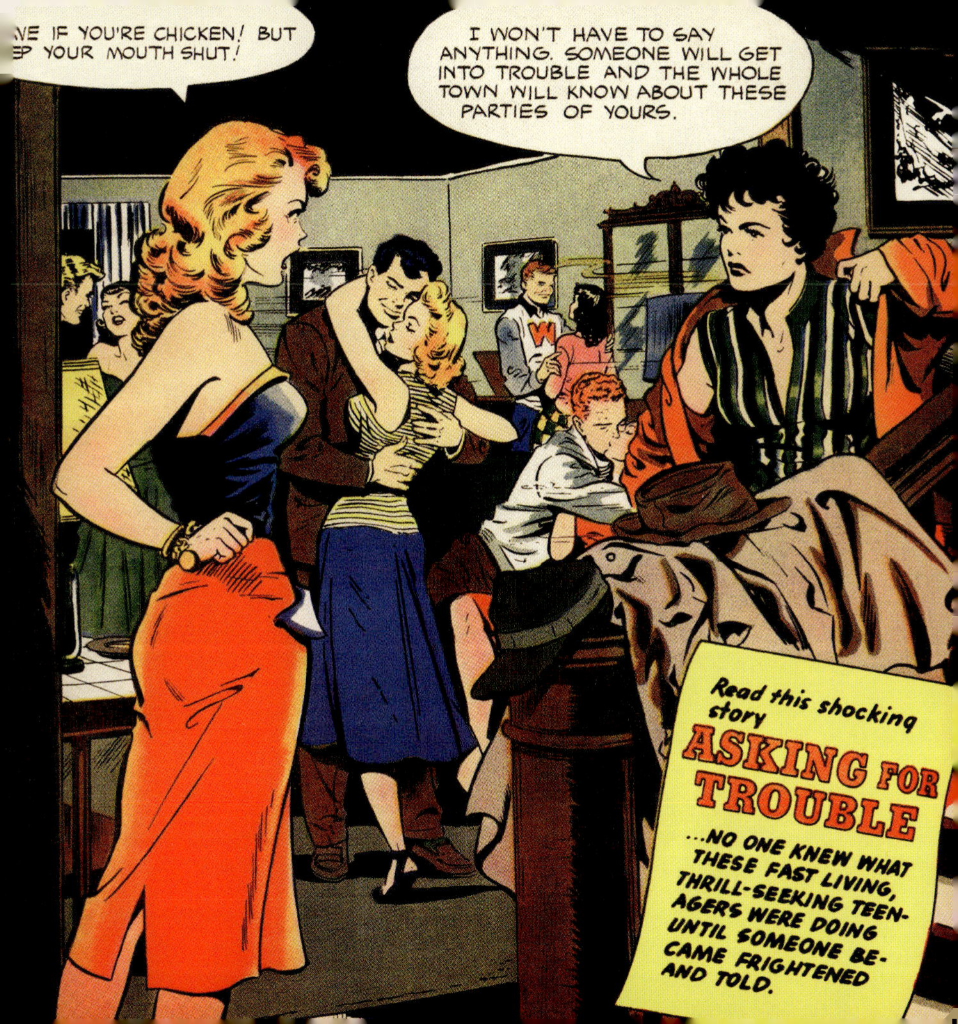

...E IF YOU'RE CHICKEN! BUT ...P YOUR MOUTH SHUT!
I WON'T HAVE TO SAY ANYTHING. SOMEONE WILL GET INTO TROUBLE AND THE WHOLE TOWN WILL KNOW ABOUT THESE PARTIES OF YOURS.
Read this shocking story
ASKING FOR TROUBLE
...NO ONE KNEW WHAT THESE FAST LIVING, THRILL-SEEKING TEEN-AGERS WERE DOING UNTIL SOMEONE BE-CAME FRIGHTENED AND TOLD.

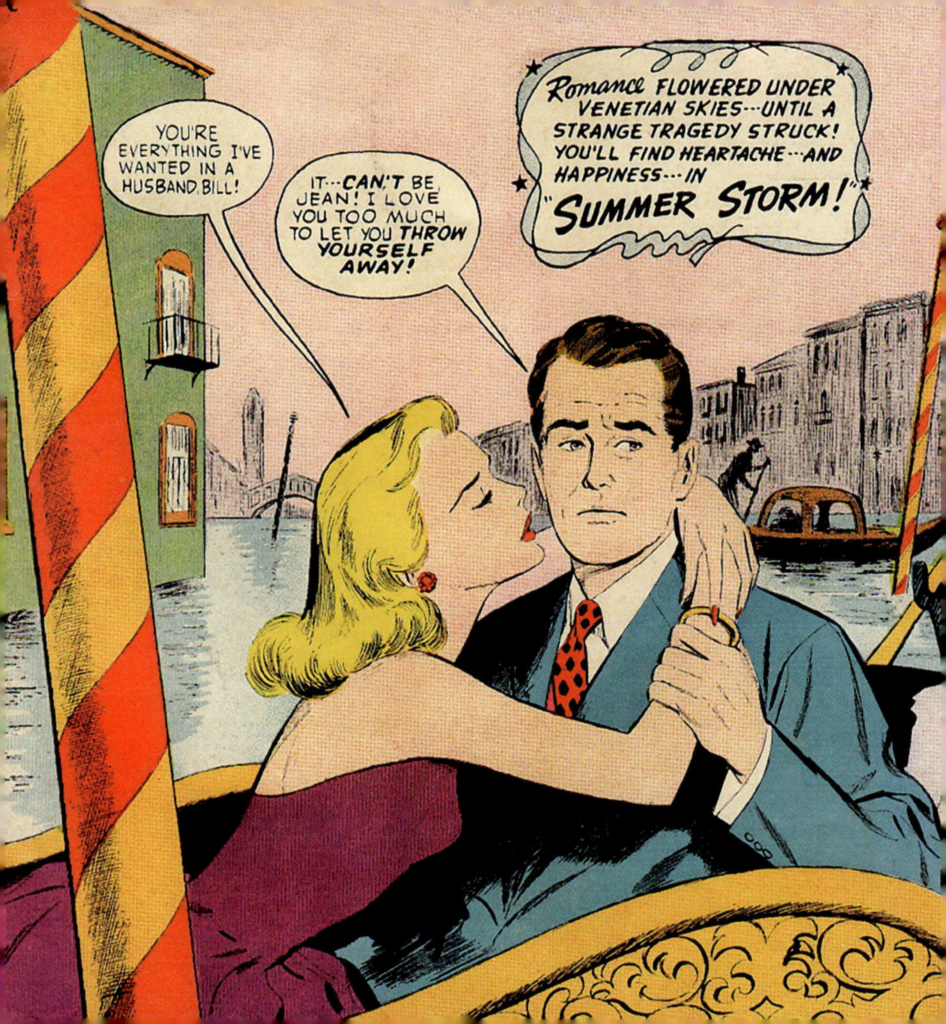
Romance FLOWERED UNDER VENETIAN SKIES---UNTIL A STRANGE TRAGEDY STRUCK! YOU'LL FIND HEARTACHE---AND HAPPINESS---IN "SUMMER STORM!"
YOU'RE EVERYTHING I'VE WANTED IN A HUSBAND, BILL!
IT---CAN'T BE, JEAN! I LOVE YOU TOO MUCH TO LET YOU THROW YOURSELF AWAY!

While Simon and Kirby are generally credited with inventing the genre in comics, historian Ron Goulart suggests in his title *Great American Comic Books* that the 1946 collection of Mary Worth newspaper reprints, *Romantic Picture Novelettes*, was in fact the very first romance comic book.

Regardless, other publishers swiftly noted Simon and Kirby's huge success and hastily released their own titles, with Timely/Marvel launching *My Romance* in August 1948, and Fox Feature Syndicate's *My Life*, the following month.

The target audience for romance comics was specifically women aged over 20, despite predominately being created by men—as seen in the incredibly sexist ending of the story *Love Without Logic*, where Sylvia has to choose between "one man [Warren, who] had everything to offer her, and was everything she had desired . . . The other [Luke] had nothing to offer her, and was everything she despised." Bizarrely, she finally decides that "Warren had talked like a philosopher . . . But Luke acted like a man! He knew that a woman may yell for equality . . . but prefers to be mastered!"

Despite these archaic masculine views they proved incredibly popular with career women whose daily dilemmas were reflected in the pulpy, four-color comics, and by 1950 there were at least 148 different titles appearing on the newsstands every month.

The general public couldn't get enough of them, and the first four years of the Fifties were a boom time with renowned artists like Matt Baker, Frank Frazetta, Leonard Starr, Alex Toth, and Wally Wood all contributing to these steamy affairs of the heart.

These "Stirring stories of real romance" followed several basic formulas:

1: I Learned My Lesson the Hard Way (but Lived Happily Ever After)

This story format was generally the most popular. A "good girl" breaks up with her safe dependable boyfriend when she falls for the "bad boy" in town. The bad boy invariably lets her down (either by chasing other women, stealing her money, or getting her in trouble with the law) and the good girl goes crawling back to her safe dependable boyfriend, who waits for her with open arms. (See: *Cast-Off Girl Friend* on page 23).

Confessions of the Lovelorn #66 (December, 1955)
Artist unknown

Bill and Jean's Venetian holiday romance is marred by a "terrible secret"—he was once a famous baseball player who broke his arm, lost his career, and is now "Drowning! Drowning in my own bitterness!" But Jean fights for their love and pulls him out of it.

2: I Learned My Lesson the Hard Way (But Didn't Live Happily Ever After)

Normally the final panel of a romance comic features the happy couple in a loving embrace. However, occasionally it all goes wrong and the main protagonists go their separate ways, older and wiser. (See: *Thrill-Crazy* on page 47).

3: A Wrongdoing is Corrected (And They Lived Happily Ever After)

In these plots, the heroine is innocent and faithful. The villain is often another woman—usually a friend, roommate, or even a sister—who schemes to destroy her rival's love life. But the duped boyfriend realizes the error of his ways and the couple are reunited. (See: *Don't Steal My Soldier* on page 24).

Nearly all romance comics follow variations based on these themes.

Women were often depicted as incomplete without a man in their lives. And the perfect man could be found just about everywhere, but they were ideally surgeons, actors, lawyers, airline pilots, or even better, the boss! And this led to endless tales of nurses, aspiring actresses, stewardesses, and secretaries wistfully thinking, "If only you knew, Earl . . . If you only knew how much I love you! I'll always love you!!" But the course of true love never did run smooth and there were plenty of "love rats," "moochers," and "wolves" for these plucky heroines to avoid as well. And, of course, there were always inscrutable "man-hungry" vamps and no-good dames ready to steal your loved one from under you.

But romance comics frequently discouraged the aggressive pursuit of men—or any behavior that even hinted at promiscuity. They would be labeled as "harlots" or "man chasers" and publically chastised and humiliated.

Female readers were encouraged—both in the stories and in the "Agony Aunt" advice columns—to maintain a passive role, and marriage and domesticity were held up as the paragons of all that was good and healthy in a relationship. Titles like *Wedding Bells*, *Just Married*, *Secrets of Young Brides*, *Brides in Love*, and *Brides Romances* actively encouraged matrimony.

When the Korean War broke out in 1950 many romance comics reflected war brides saying goodbye to their beaus in titles such as *G.I. Sweethearts* and *True War Romances*. In fact, there

Teen-Age Romances #15 (April, 1951)
Matt Baker

Written by Dana Dutch and drawn by Matt Baker, *I was an Army Camp Pick-Up* has Marlene simultaneously playing the field and trashing her reputation.

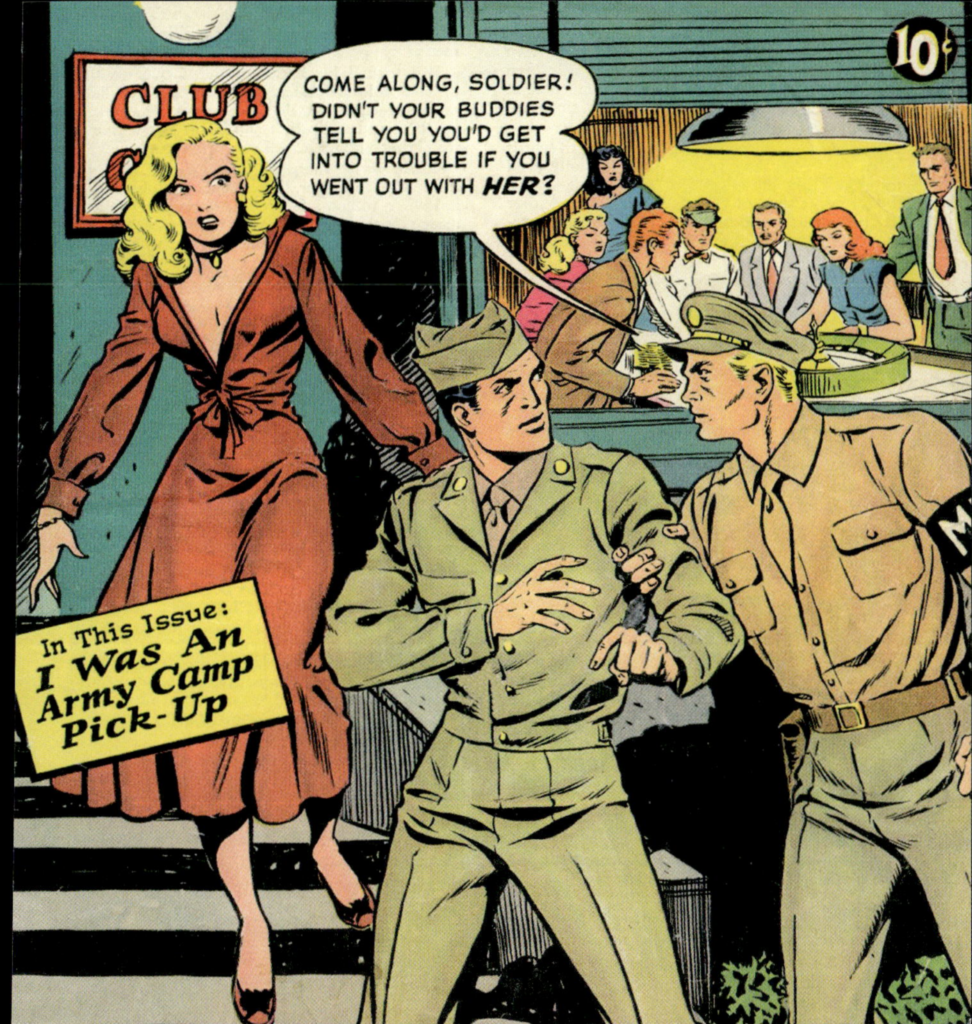
10¢
CLUB
COME ALONG, SOLDIER! DIDN'T YOUR BUDDIES TELL YOU YOU'D GET INTO TROUBLE IF YOU WENT OUT WITH HER?
In This Issue: I Was An Army Camp Pick-Up

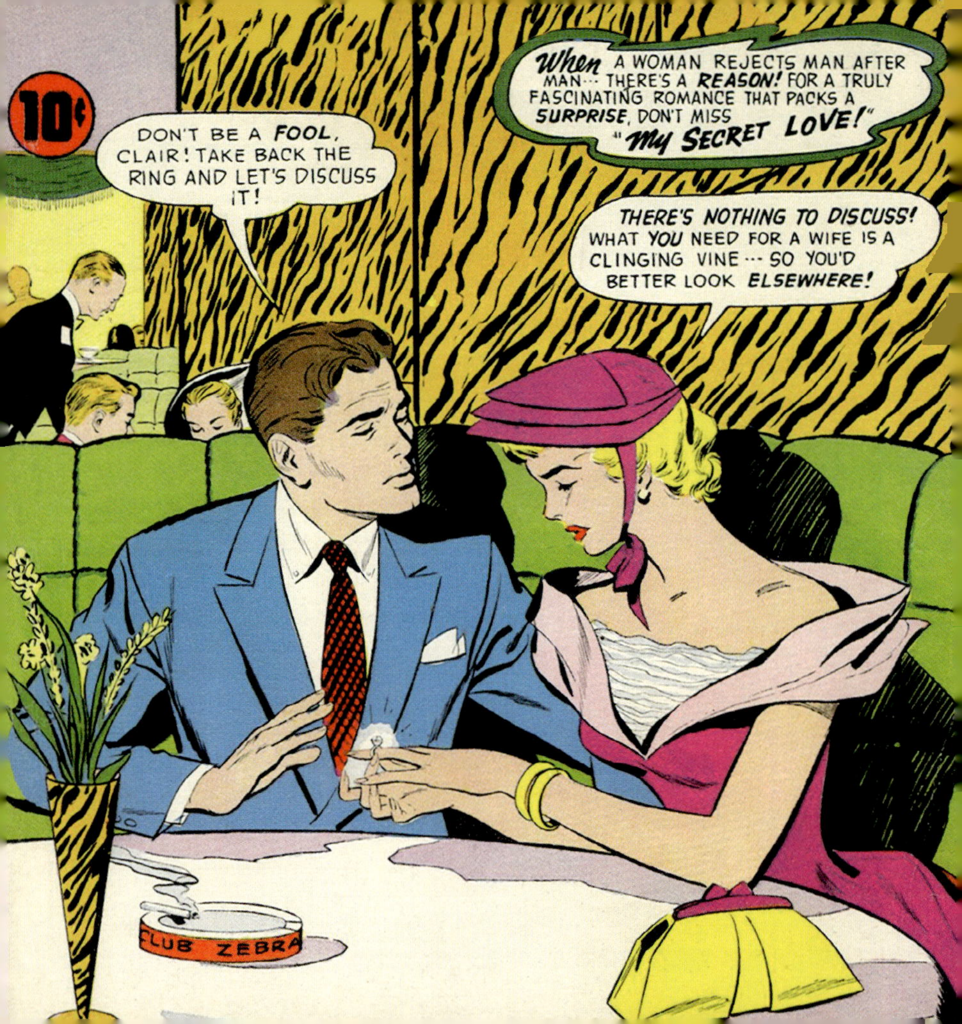
10¢
WHEN A WOMAN REJECTS MAN AFTER MAN... THERE'S A REASON! FOR A TRULY FASCINATING ROMANCE THAT PACKS A SURPRISE, DON'T MISS "MY SECRET LOVE!"
DON'T BE A FOOL, CLAIR! TAKE BACK THE RING AND LET'S DISCUSS IT!
THERE'S NOTHING TO DISCUSS! WHAT YOU NEED FOR A WIFE IS A CLINGING VINE... SO YOU'D BETTER LOOK ELSEWHERE!
CLUB ZEBRA

were romance comics to suit all tastes and sectors of society from a glut of western romances such as *Cowboy Romance*, *Range Romances*, *Cowgirl Romances*, and *Western Life Romances* to *Hi-School Romance*, *Teen-Age Romances*, and *Negro Romance*, the last published by Fawcett.

The popularity of romance comics ate into the sales of confession magazines like *True Story* and *Confidential*, and not everyone was enamored with them. The August 22, 1949 issue of *Time* magazine reported that love comics were "outselling all others, even the blood and thunder variety... For pulp magazines, the moral was even clearer: no matter how low their standards for fiction, the comics could find lower ones."

By 1954, romance comics, like all genres, were about to suffer the great "comic purges"—spearheaded by child psychologist, Dr. Frederic Wertham, and enacted by parents, teachers, clergymen, and other "concerned citizens." The general assumption was that comic books were contributing to American juvenile delinquency. Ignoring the fact that the majority of romance comics were, in fact, targeted at older female readers—as evidenced by the endless ads for make-up, panty girdles, dresses, and pimple and bust creams—Wertham attacked the comics for their "Mushiness... social hypocrisy... false sentiments... cheapness," and "... titillation." He believed that romance comics presented female readers false images of love and contributed to feelings of physical inferiority.

When the Comics Code was introduced later that year publishers self-censored their titles. Romance comics had always been deeply moralistic anyway, but now all the spice that had made them appealing had been removed, making the stories incredibly bland and innocent—if not naive—with a heavy emphasis on outmoded patriarchal values of gender roles, domesticity, and marriage.

The final nail in the coffin for the genre came with the sexual revolution of the 1960s. No longer were women's sole concerns about finding the ideal "dream boat" to marry, settle down with, and be a good housewife. They wanted more than the comics could deliver.

As the late Charlton and DC Comics artist and editor Dick Giordano recalled in 2005: "Girls simply outgrew romance comics... [The content was] too tame for the more sophisticated, sexually liberated... women's libbers were able to see nudity, strong sexual content—and life the way it really was—in other media. Hand-holding and

---

My Romantic Adventures #56 (June, 1955)
Kenneth Bald

This quite modern cover for the story, *My Secret Love* rejects the usual simpering female for a tougher protaganist, demanding more equal status.

pining after the cute boy on the football team just didn't do it anymore, and the Comics Code wouldn't pass anything that truly resembled real-life relationships."

Charlton Comics tried to capture this new zeitgeist with titles like *Career Girl Romance* (launched in 1964), but it failed to reignite a disinterested readership. DC, Marvel, and Charlton Comics all continued to publish a few limp romance titles into the mid-Seventies, but the genre never regained the popular heights it had once soared to.

The Golden Age of romance comics came to an end with the last issue of *Young Romance* #208 in 1975 (the very title that started the boom back in 1947). The cover implied a racy—and very modern—ménage à trois: "Did I have to give up the girl I loved for the boy I loved?" With the boy demanding: "I'm offering you my love, Darling! That means Debbie can't tag along with us anymore!" And his weeping girlfriend replying: "You don't know what it's like being alone! I won't give her up!" Typically, the interiors failed to live up to the sexual frisson promised on the front.

Finally, the other long-running romance title, *Young Love*, ended with #126 in July, 1977, featuring the banner, "Was distance the only thing that kept alive the C.B. Romance?" It was evident that "Today's Young Women" had moved on, and not even C.B. radio romances were ever going to bring them back.

Sweetheart Diary #65 (August, 1962)
Charles Nicholas and Vincent Alascia

Cynthia Doyle is secretly a "Nurse in Love" with dashing surgeon Dr. Edward Benson, in *Diagnosis: Heartbreak*. They eventually fall madly in love, but not without their fair share of heartache along the way. Fortunately, Dr. Benson has the cure for Cynthia's lovesick blues.

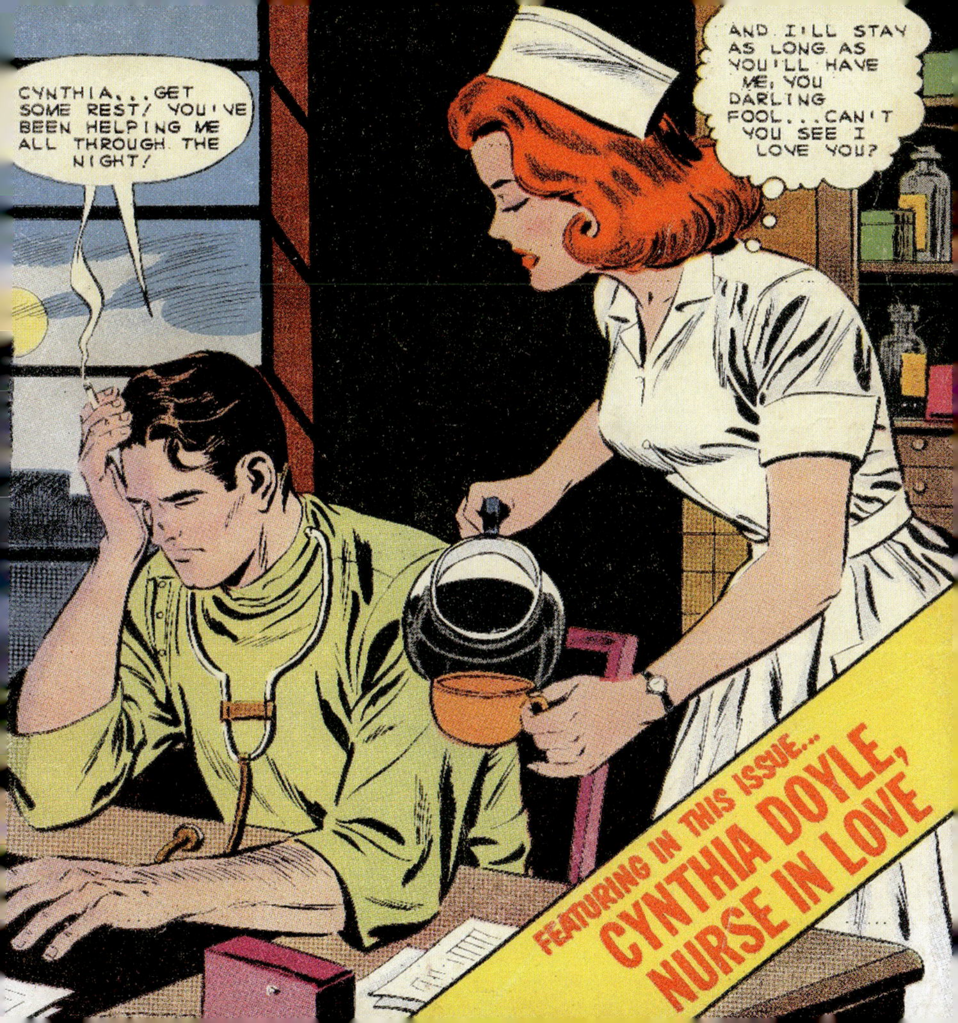
CYNTHIA...GET SOME REST! YOU'VE BEEN HELPING ME ALL THROUGH THE NIGHT!
AND I'LL STAY AS LONG AS YOU'LL HAVE ME, YOU DARLING FOOL...CAN'T YOU SEE I LOVE YOU?
FEATURING IN THIS ISSUE...
CYNTHIA DOYLE, NURSE IN LOVE

The Magnets and the Stories Behind Them

Hi-School Romance #13 (February, 1952)
Artist unknown

In *A Marriage Made in Heaven* Rose's world is turned upside down when her parents are killed in a plane crash in front of her. Leaving her American boyfriend Marty she returns to Mexico to live with her grandfather. There she meets Latin Lothario Manuelo Sanchez, "You needn't be coy with me now, my Rosita! Our marriage is arranged!" Sanchez then attempts to woo his betrothed. Offended, Rose uses Marty, who's visiting, to get even with the arrogant Manuelo. But when the Mexican is hurt in a game of Jai-Lai she rushes to his side and he becomes humbled, "Oh my dear one . . . I have been a fool! I love you, Rosita . . . Will you marry me . . . Please?" "Yes!! Of course I will . . . Now that you've asked me . . . Not told me!!" Poor old Marty.

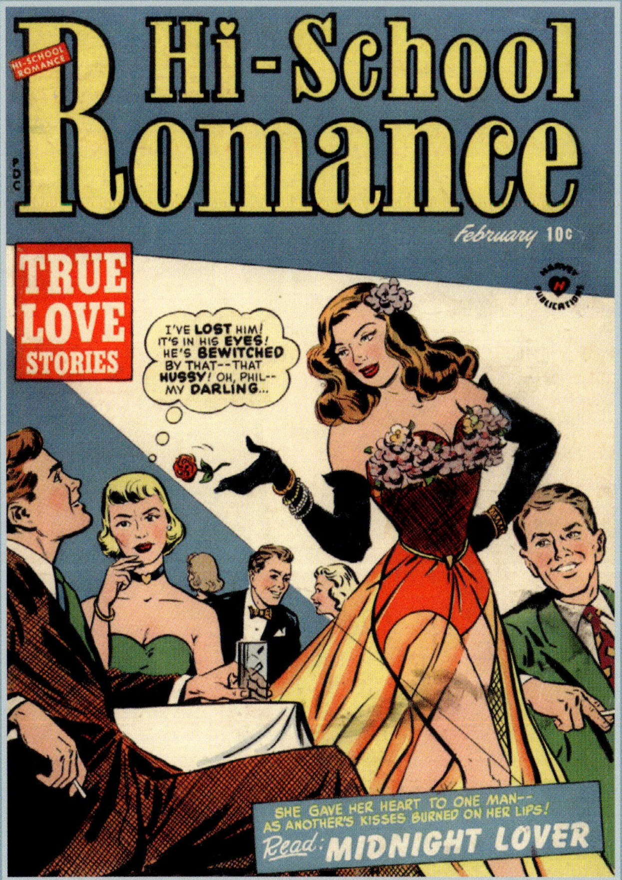

HI-SCHOOL ROMANCE
P.D.C.
Hi-School Romance
February 10¢
HARVEY PUBLICATIONS
TRUE LOVE STORIES
I'VE LOST HIM! IT'S IN HIS EYES! HE'S BEWITCHED BY THAT--THAT HUSSY! OH, PHIL-- MY DARLING...
SHE GAVE HER HEART TO ONE MAN-- AS ANOTHER'S KISSES BURNED ON HER LIPS!
Read: MIDNIGHT LOVER

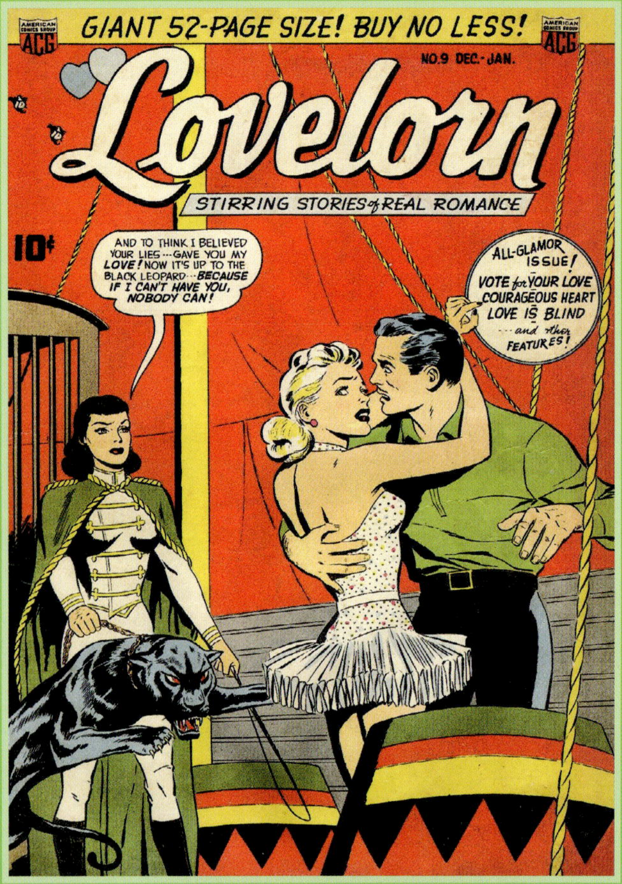
GIANT 52-PAGE SIZE! BUY NO LESS!
AMERICAN COMICS GROUP ACG
NO.9 DEC.-JAN.
Lovelorn
STIRRING STORIES of REAL ROMANCE
10¢
AND TO THINK I BELIEVED YOUR LIES---GAVE YOU MY LOVE! NOW IT'S UP TO THE BLACK LEOPARD---BECAUSE IF I CAN'T HAVE YOU, NOBODY CAN!
ALL-GLAMOR ISSUE! VOTE for YOUR LOVE COURAGEOUS HEART LOVE IS BLIND ---and other FEATURES!

***Lovelorn* #9 (December-January, 1950-1951)**
Artist unknown

Hell hath no fury like Lora Morelli—"Queen of the Big Top!"—scorned, in *Courageous Heart*. Lora runs a big-cat act at the circus and longs for a man to love, but rejects artist Tom for being "Spineless . . . Weak!" when they are almost attacked by an escaped lion. Instead she falls in love with the arrogant aerialist animal-baiter Lopez instead. But her world falls apart when she catches Lopez, "two-timing with that stupid little flirt Clarabelle!" Things take a turn for a worse when Lopez's taunting of Satan causes the panther to attack Lora and "Maul her a bit . . ." Her nerves shot and her career in tatters she finally realizes that true love lies in the arms of the gentle Tom: " . . . I've no pride left! All I have is a woman's heart . . . And it's beating for you! Please give me a chance!" The painter replies, "Honey, I've been waiting to hear that!"

Heart Throbs #33 (March, 1955)
Artist unknown

"I fell in love with Andy the moment I met him! But being his girl meant giving up my friends and all the good times that go with a high school crowd! I couldn't give him up and yet our love was hopeless because I was *Too Young to Make Plans*." Thus begins Gwen's tale of woe. She's 17 and he's a mature 22-year-old, and Andy's disdain for Gwen's pals tears them apart, "Those girls! There can't be a brain in their heads! All they did was giggle and make fools of themselves! And the boys! They ought to be out playing marbles instead of dating girls!" After splitting up, Gwen tries dating boys her own age but "*sob* I don't fit in with the kids anymore! *sob* All evening long I kept thinking of Andy . . ." Happily the star-crossed lovers are reunited and Andy proposes marriage, "Does that sound grown up to you?" "Not when you hold me close like this, Andy!" simpers Gwen. "And when you kiss me, I think I'll even be able to name the date!"

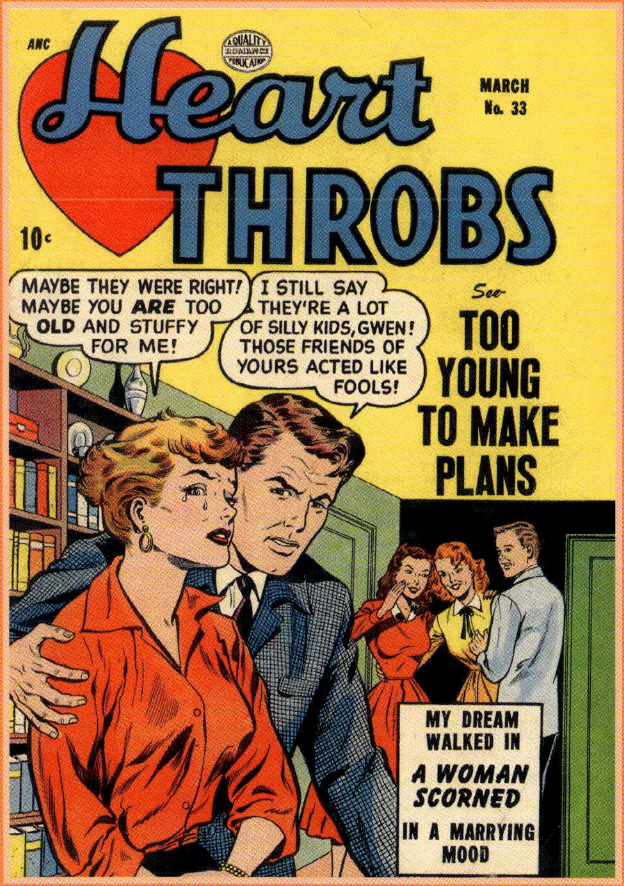

ANC
Heart THROBS
QUALITY ROMANCE PUBLICATION
MARCH
No. 33
10¢
MAYBE THEY WERE RIGHT! MAYBE YOU ARE TOO OLD AND STUFFY FOR ME!
I STILL SAY THEY'RE A LOT OF SILLY KIDS, GWEN! THOSE FRIENDS OF YOURS ACTED LIKE FOOLS!
See- TOO YOUNG TO MAKE PLANS
MY DREAM WALKED IN
A WOMAN SCORNED
IN A MARRYING MOOD

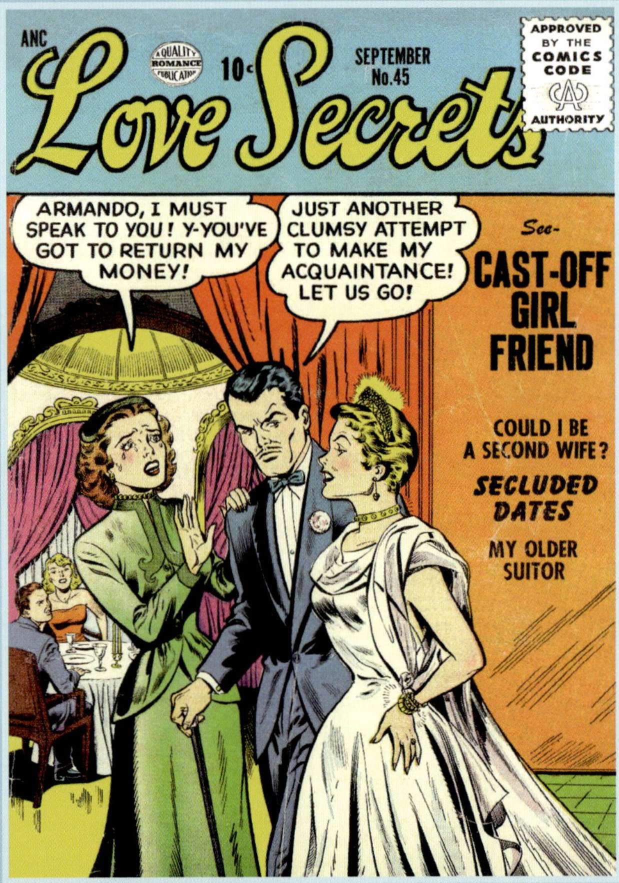
ANC
Love Secrets
A QUALITY ROMANCE PUBLICATION
10¢
SEPTEMBER
No.45
APPROVED BY THE COMICS CODE AUTHORITY
ARMANDO, I MUST SPEAK TO YOU! Y-YOU'VE GOT TO RETURN MY MONEY!
JUST ANOTHER CLUMSY ATTEMPT TO MAKE MY ACQUAINTANCE! LET US GO!
See-
CAST-OFF GIRL FRIEND
COULD I BE A SECOND WIFE?
SECLUDED DATES
MY OLDER SUITOR

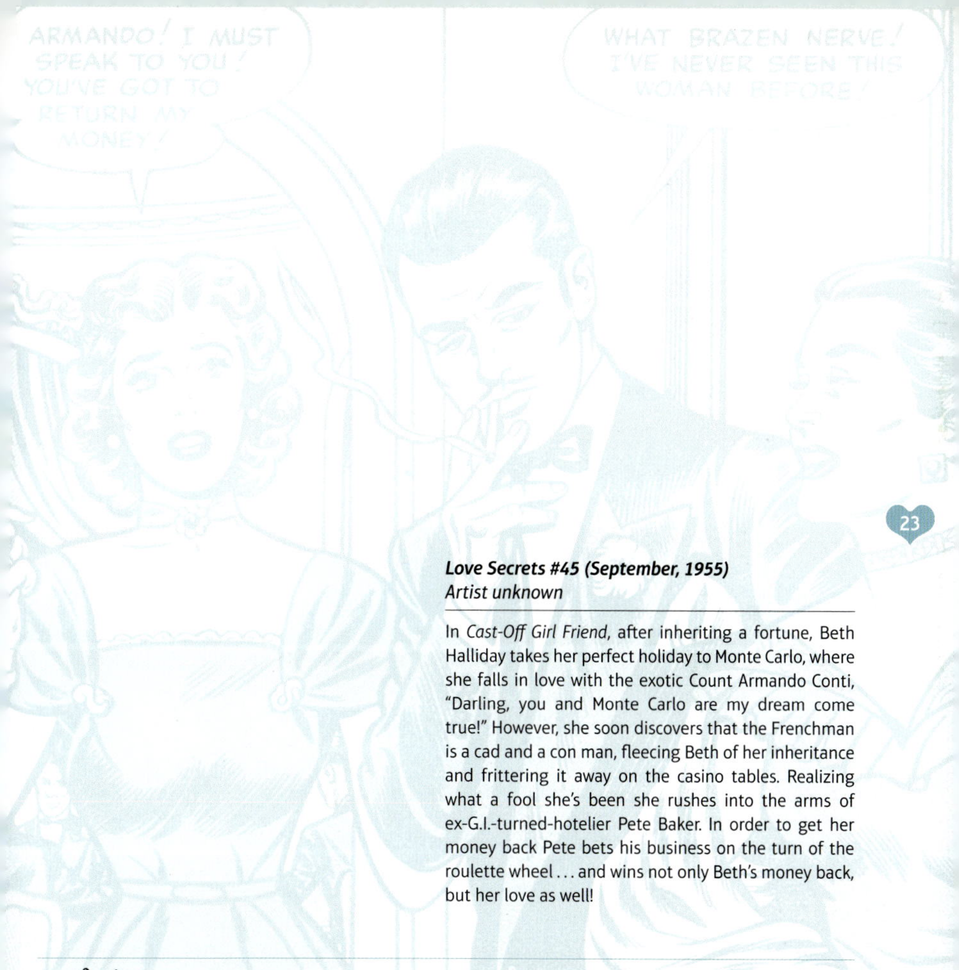
ARMANDO! I MUST SPEAK TO YOU! YOU'VE GOT TO RETURN MY MONEY!
WHAT BRAZEN NERVE! I'VE NEVER SEEN THIS WOMAN BEFORE!

Love Secrets #45 (September, 1955)
Artist unknown

In *Cast-Off Girl Friend*, after inheriting a fortune, Beth Halliday takes her perfect holiday to Monte Carlo, where she falls in love with the exotic Count Armando Conti, "Darling, you and Monte Carlo are my dream come true!" However, she soon discovers that the Frenchman is a cad and a con man, fleecing Beth of her inheritance and frittering it away on the casino tables. Realizing what a fool she's been she rushes into the arms of ex-G.I.-turned-hotelier Pete Baker. In order to get her money back Pete bets his business on the turn of the roulette wheel . . . and wins not only Beth's money back, but her love as well!

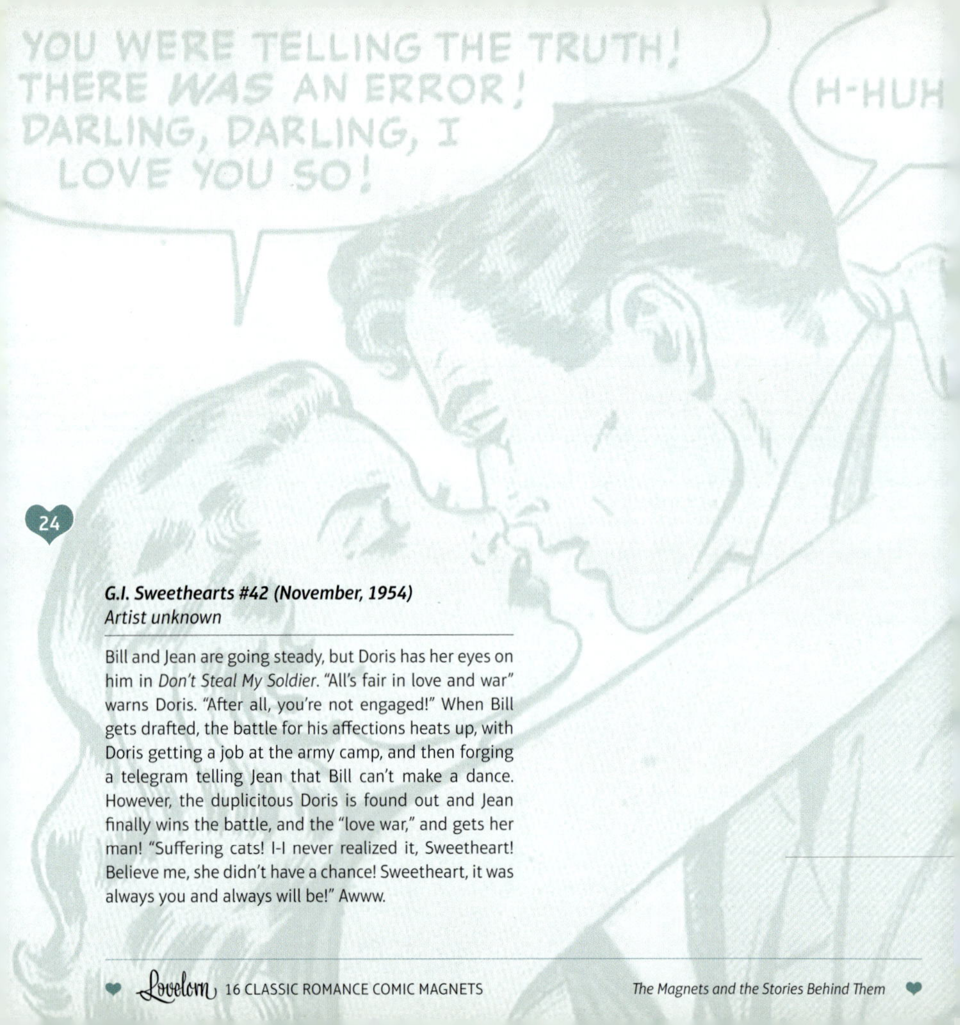
YOU WERE TELLING THE TRUTH! THERE WAS AN ERROR! DARLING, DARLING, I LOVE YOU SO!
H-HUH

G.I. Sweethearts #42 (November, 1954)
Artist unknown

Bill and Jean are going steady, but Doris has her eyes on him in *Don't Steal My Soldier*. "All's fair in love and war" warns Doris. "After all, you're not engaged!" When Bill gets drafted, the battle for his affections heats up, with Doris getting a job at the army camp, and then forging a telegram telling Jean that Bill can't make a dance. However, the duplicitous Doris is found out and Jean finally wins the battle, and the "love war," and gets her man! "Suffering cats! I-I never realized it, Sweetheart! Believe me, she didn't have a chance! Sweetheart, it was always you and always will be!" Awww.

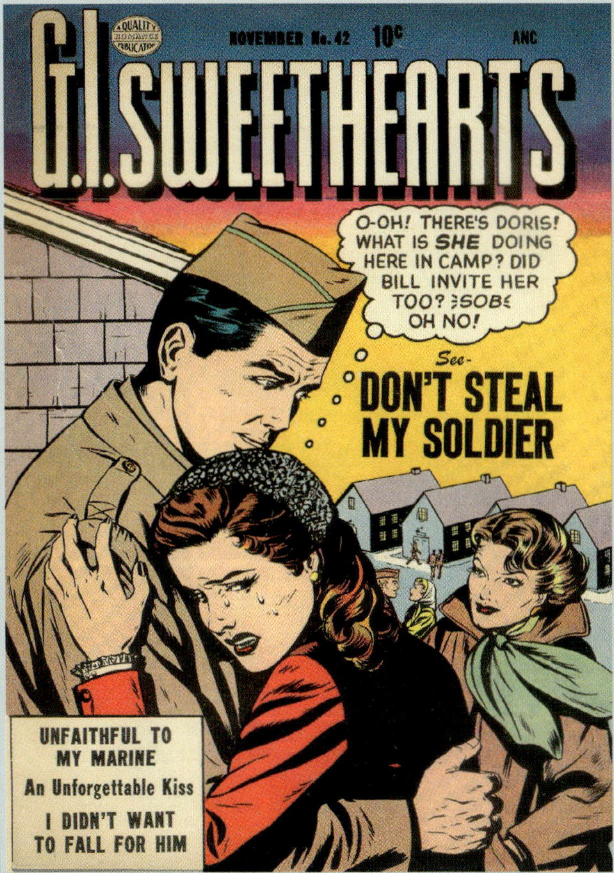
G.I. SWEETHEARTS
QUALITY ROMANCE PUBLICATION
NOVEMBER No. 42
10¢
ANC
O-OH! THERE'S DORIS! WHAT IS SHE DOING HERE IN CAMP? DID BILL INVITE HER TOO? SOB OH NO!
See-
DON'T STEAL MY SOLDIER
UNFAITHFUL TO MY MARINE
An Unforgettable Kiss
I DIDN'T WANT TO FALL FOR HIM

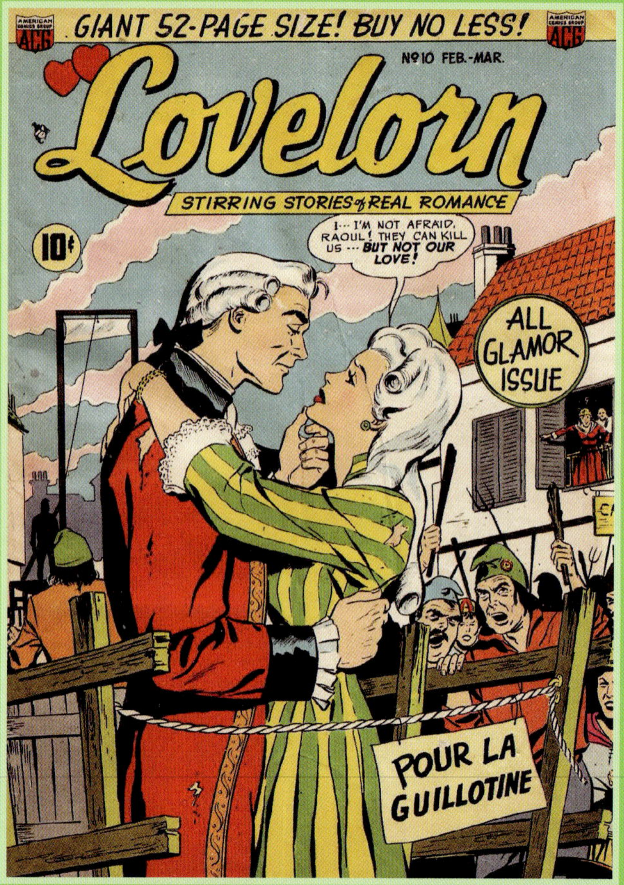

ACG
GIANT 52-PAGE SIZE! BUY NO LESS!
ACG
No 10 FEB.-MAR.
Lovelorn
STIRRING STORIES of REAL ROMANCE
10¢
I-- I'M NOT AFRAID, RAOUL! THEY CAN KILL US --- BUT NOT OUR LOVE!
ALL GLAMOR ISSUE
POUR LA GUILLOTINE

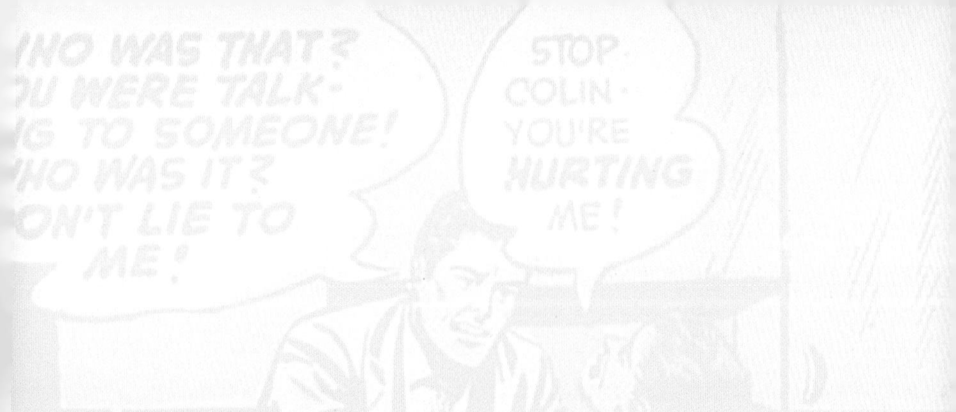
STOP COLIN YOU'RE HURTING ME!

Lovelorn #10 (February-March, 1951)
Artist unknown

This scene doesn't appear anywhere in the comic, but it perfectly sums up the romantic ideal in the face of adversity! Instead, the stories inside include *You Belong to Me!*, a tale of the hugely jealous Janet whose obsessive behavior drives her fiancé away. When she goes on holiday to her aunt's to recover from the break-up she meets, and falls in love with, Colin. However, Colin turns out to be even more possessive than Janet, driving her to tears. "You . . . You can't own another person, Colin . . . You want to imprison me. To shut off the rest of the world . . . and that's impossible!" In a final, perverted twist, Janet's aunt reveals that the entire relationship with Colin has been some sick family psychotherapy role-play to make her see the error of her ways, "Bravo! Bravo! . . . Your mother wrote me about your engagement, Janet! And she asked me to help you, if I could! But you helped yourself . . . And that's the best way to learn!"

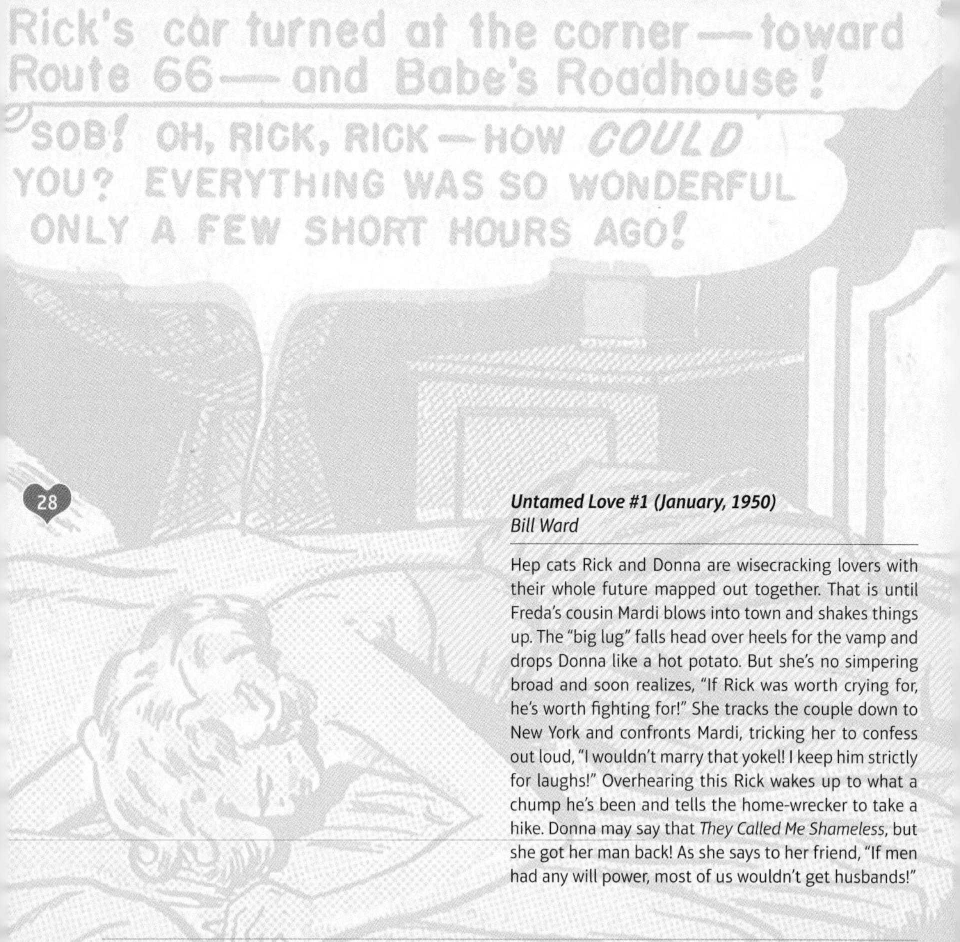
Rick's car turned at the corner — toward Route 66 — and Babe's Roadhouse!
SOB! OH, RICK, RICK — HOW COULD YOU? EVERYTHING WAS SO WONDERFUL ONLY A FEW SHORT HOURS AGO!

Untamed Love #1 (January, 1950)
Bill Ward

Hep cats Rick and Donna are wisecracking lovers with their whole future mapped out together. That is until Freda's cousin Mardi blows into town and shakes things up. The "big lug" falls head over heels for the vamp and drops Donna like a hot potato. But she's no simpering broad and soon realizes, "If Rick was worth crying for, he's worth fighting for!" She tracks the couple down to New York and confronts Mardi, tricking her to confess out loud, "I wouldn't marry that yokel! I keep him strictly for laughs!" Overhearing this Rick wakes up to what a chump he's been and tells the home-wrecker to take a hike. Donna may say that *They Called Me Shameless*, but she got her man back! As she says to her friend, "If men had any will power, most of us wouldn't get husbands!"

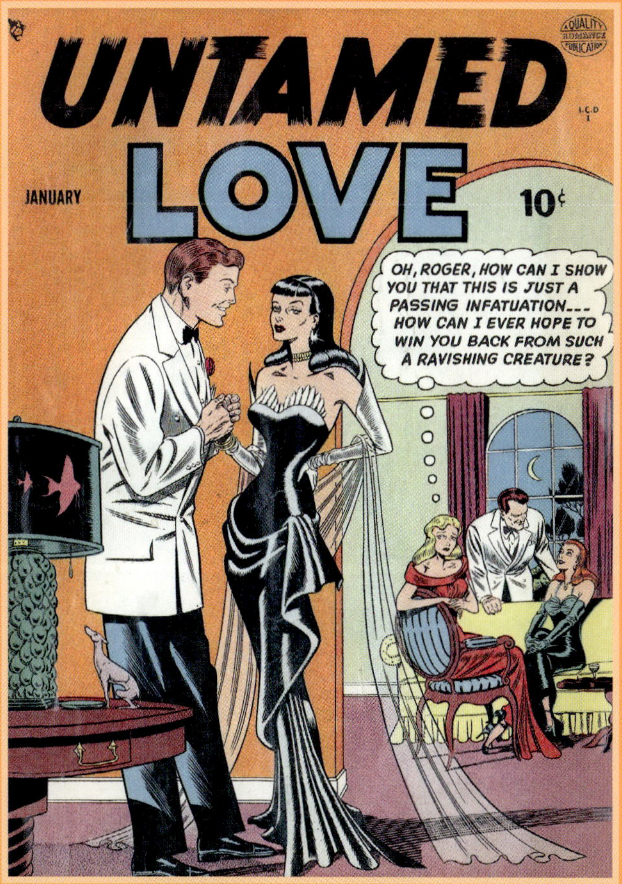
UNTAMED LOVE
A QUALITY ROMANCE PUBLICATION
JANUARY
10¢
OH, ROGER, HOW CAN I SHOW YOU THAT THIS IS JUST A PASSING INFATUATION--- HOW CAN I EVER HOPE TO WIN YOU BACK FROM SUCH A RAVISHING CREATURE?

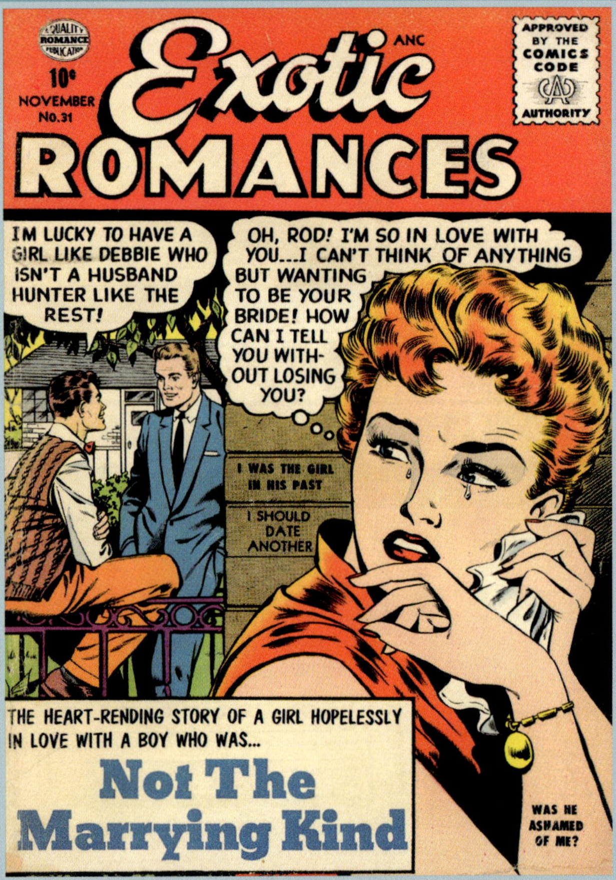

QUALITY ROMANCE PUBLICATION
10¢
NOVEMBER
No.31
Exotic ROMANCES
ANC
APPROVED BY THE COMICS CODE AUTHORITY
IM LUCKY TO HAVE A GIRL LIKE DEBBIE WHO ISN'T A HUSBAND HUNTER LIKE THE REST!
OH, ROD! I'M SO IN LOVE WITH YOU...I CAN'T THINK OF ANYTHING BUT WANTING TO BE YOUR BRIDE! HOW CAN I TELL YOU WITH-OUT LOSING YOU?
I WAS THE GIRL IN HIS PAST
I SHOULD DATE ANOTHER
THE HEART-RENDING STORY OF A GIRL HOPELESSLY IN LOVE WITH A BOY WHO WAS...
Not The Marrying Kind
WAS HE ASHAMED OF ME?

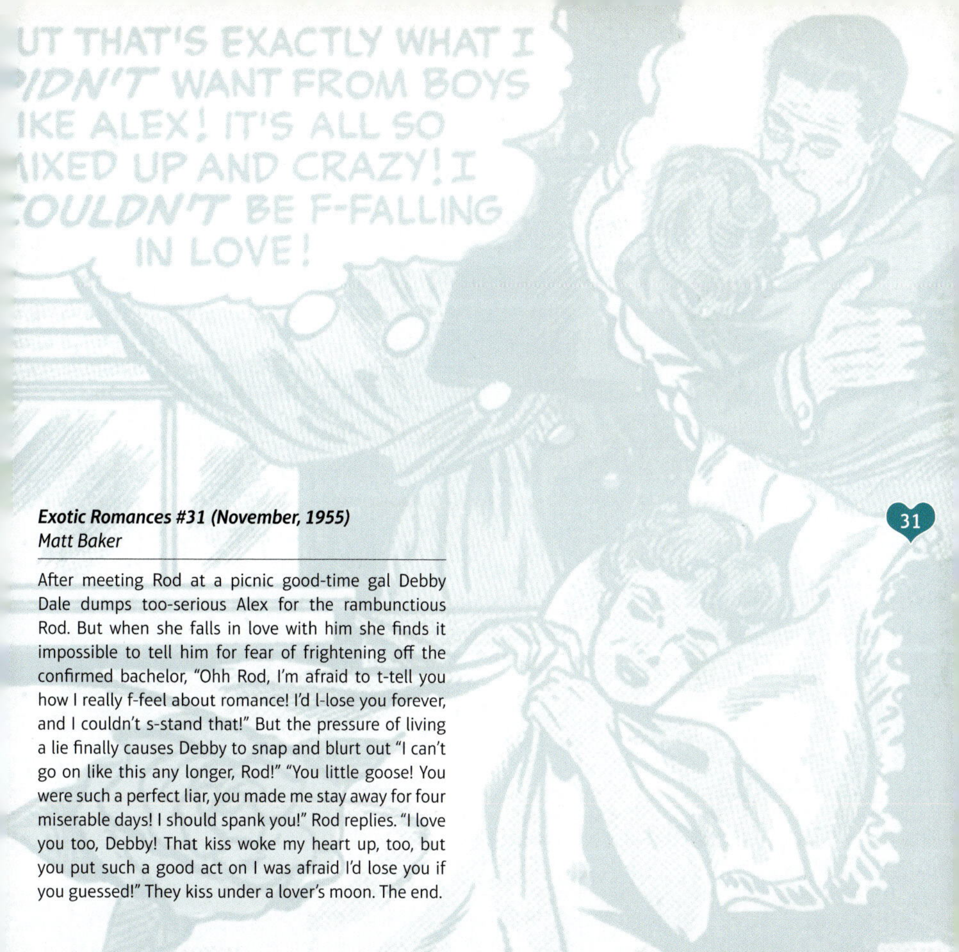
UT THAT'S EXACTLY WHAT I
IDN'T WANT FROM BOYS
IKE ALEX! IT'S ALL SO
IXED UP AND CRAZY! I
OULDN'T BE F-FALLING
IN LOVE!

Exotic Romances #31 (November, 1955)
Matt Baker

After meeting Rod at a picnic good-time gal Debby Dale dumps too-serious Alex for the rambunctious Rod. But when she falls in love with him she finds it impossible to tell him for fear of frightening off the confirmed bachelor, "Ohh Rod, I'm afraid to t-tell you how I really f-feel about romance! I'd l-lose you forever, and I couldn't s-stand that!" But the pressure of living a lie finally causes Debby to snap and blurt out "I can't go on like this any longer, Rod!" "You little goose! You were such a perfect liar, you made me stay away for four miserable days! I should spank you!" Rod replies. "I love you too, Debby! That kiss woke my heart up, too, but you put such a good act on I was afraid I'd lose you if you guessed!" They kiss under a lover's moon. The end.

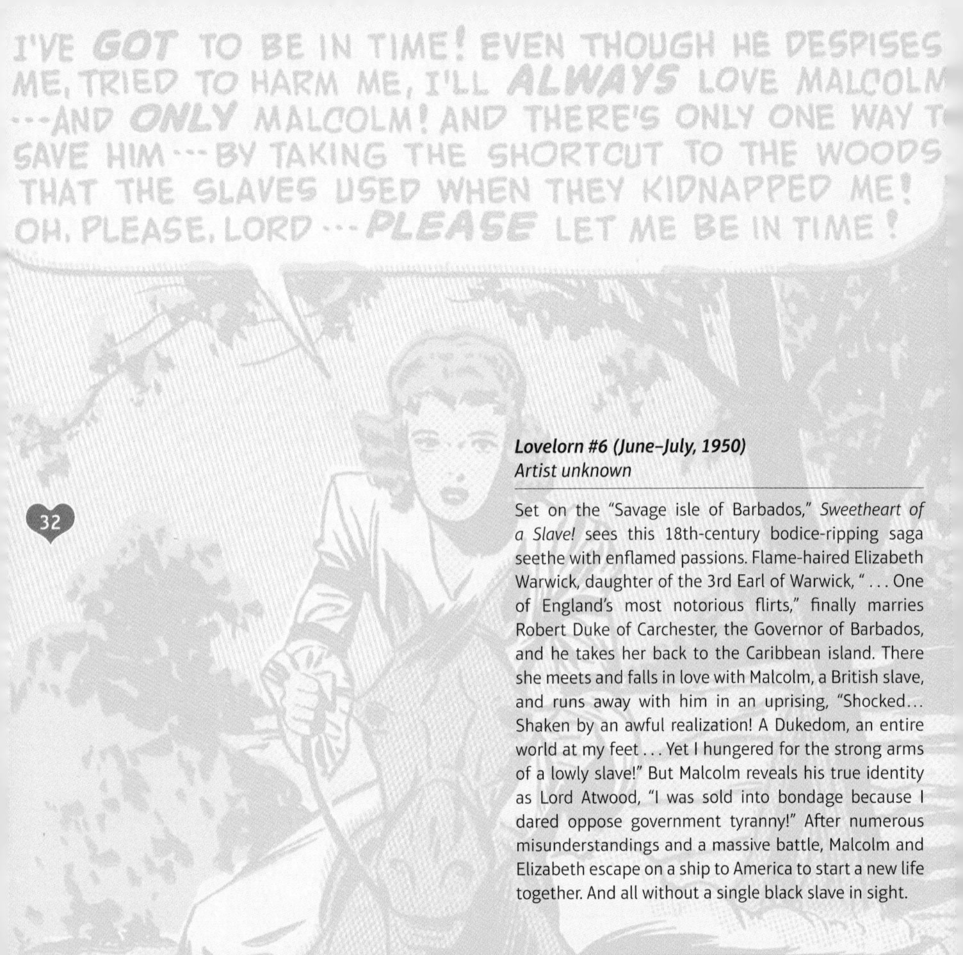
I'VE GOT TO BE IN TIME! EVEN THOUGH HE DESPISES ME, TRIED TO HARM ME, I'LL ALWAYS LOVE MALCOLM ---AND ONLY MALCOLM! AND THERE'S ONLY ONE WAY T SAVE HIM---BY TAKING THE SHORTCUT TO THE WOODS THAT THE SLAVES USED WHEN THEY KIDNAPPED ME! OH, PLEASE, LORD---PLEASE LET ME BE IN TIME!

Lovelorn #6 (June–July, 1950)
Artist unknown

Set on the "Savage isle of Barbados," *Sweetheart of a Slave!* sees this 18th-century bodice-ripping saga seethe with enflamed passions. Flame-haired Elizabeth Warwick, daughter of the 3rd Earl of Warwick, " . . . One of England's most notorious flirts," finally marries Robert Duke of Carchester, the Governor of Barbados, and he takes her back to the Caribbean island. There she meets and falls in love with Malcolm, a British slave, and runs away with him in an uprising, "Shocked… Shaken by an awful realization! A Dukedom, an entire world at my feet . . . Yet I hungered for the strong arms of a lowly slave!" But Malcolm reveals his true identity as Lord Atwood, "I was sold into bondage because I dared oppose government tyranny!" After numerous misunderstandings and a massive battle, Malcolm and Elizabeth escape on a ship to America to start a new life together. And all without a single black slave in sight.

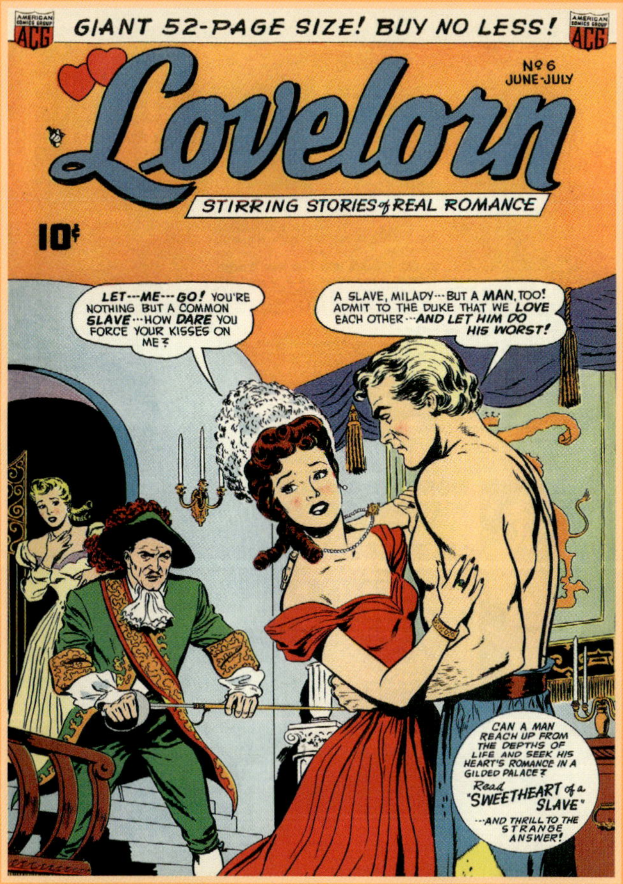

GIANT 52-PAGE SIZE! BUY NO LESS!
AMERICAN COMICS GROUP ACG
Nº 6 JUNE-JULY
Lovelorn
STIRRING STORIES of REAL ROMANCE
10¢
LET---ME---GO! YOU'RE NOTHING BUT A COMMON SLAVE---HOW DARE YOU FORCE YOUR KISSES ON ME?
A SLAVE, MILADY---BUT A MAN, TOO! ADMIT TO THE DUKE THAT WE LOVE EACH OTHER---AND LET HIM DO HIS WORST!
CAN A MAN REACH UP FROM THE DEPTHS OF LIFE AND SEEK HIS HEART'S ROMANCE IN A GILDED PALACE? Read "SWEETHEART of a SLAVE" ---AND THRILL TO THE STRANGE ANSWER!

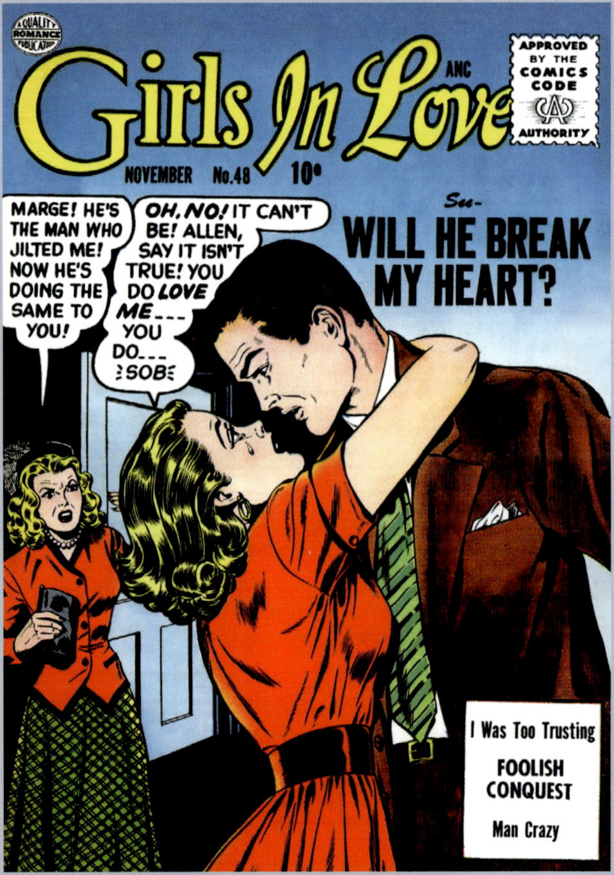
A QUALITY ROMANCE PUBLICATION
Girls In Love
ANC
APPROVED BY THE COMICS CODE AUTHORITY
NOVEMBER No.48 10¢
MARGE! HE'S THE MAN WHO JILTED ME! NOW HE'S DOING THE SAME TO YOU!
OH, NO! IT CAN'T BE! ALLEN, SAY IT ISN'T TRUE! YOU DO LOVE ME--- YOU DO--- SOB
See-
WILL HE BREAK MY HEART?
I Was Too Trusting
FOOLISH CONQUEST
Man Crazy

Girls in Love #48 (November, 1955)
Artist unknown

Marge thought, "Allen Lane was the finest, kindest, most wonderful man in the world and I gladly gave him my heart! Then I discovered the shocking truth! Allen was the man who had run out on my best girl friend! How will I know I won't share the same fate? Does he really love me or *Will He Break My Heart?*" But it turns out that Allen left Linda at the altar because she was cheating on him! "Sure I was running around with Pete, but Allen didn't have to make such a scene!" When the truth comes out Marge grabs Allen, "As our lips met I realized the chains that bound our hearts together had never really been broken at all! There could never be anyone for me but Allen!"

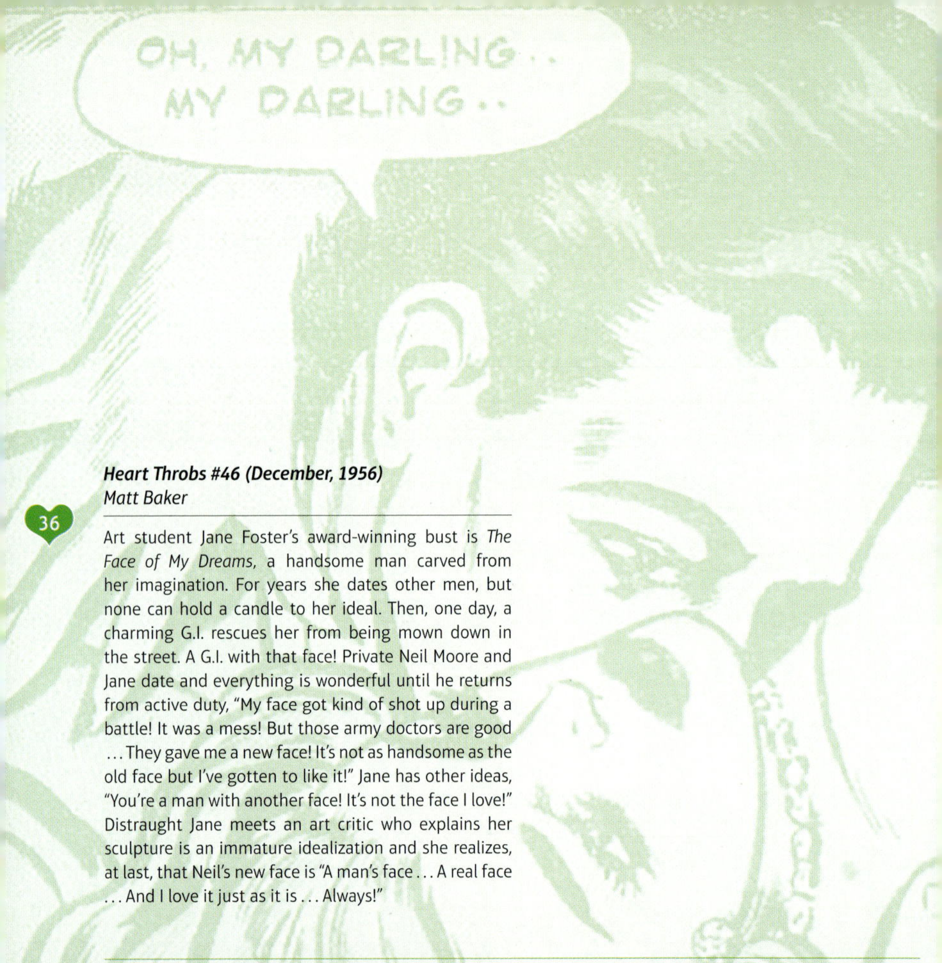
OH, MY DARLING..
MY DARLING..

Heart Throbs #46 (December, 1956)
Matt Baker

Art student Jane Foster's award-winning bust is *The Face of My Dreams*, a handsome man carved from her imagination. For years she dates other men, but none can hold a candle to her ideal. Then, one day, a charming G.I. rescues her from being mown down in the street. A G.I. with that face! Private Neil Moore and Jane date and everything is wonderful until he returns from active duty, "My face got kind of shot up during a battle! It was a mess! But those army doctors are good . . . They gave me a new face! It's not as handsome as the old face but I've gotten to like it!" Jane has other ideas, "You're a man with another face! It's not the face I love!" Distraught Jane meets an art critic who explains her sculpture is an immature idealization and she realizes, at last, that Neil's new face is "A man's face . . . A real face . . . And I love it just as it is . . . Always!"

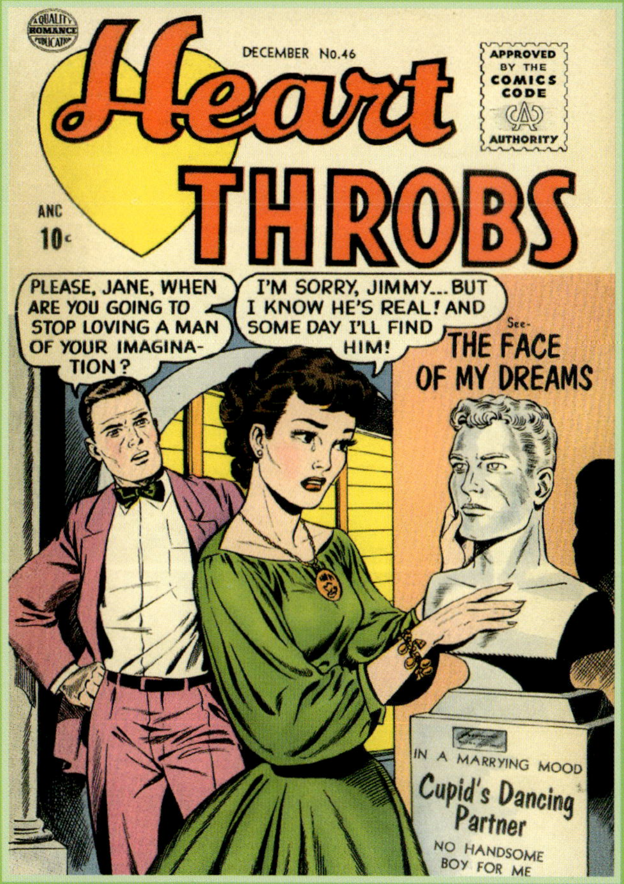
A QUALITY ROMANCE PUBLICATION
Heart THROBS
DECEMBER No.46
APPROVED BY THE COMICS CODE AUTHORITY
ANC
10¢
PLEASE, JANE, WHEN ARE YOU GOING TO STOP LOVING A MAN OF YOUR IMAGINATION?
I'M SORRY, JIMMY... BUT I KNOW HE'S REAL! AND SOME DAY I'LL FIND HIM!
See- THE FACE OF MY DREAMS
IN A MARRYING MOOD
Cupid's Dancing Partner
NO HANDSOME BOY FOR ME

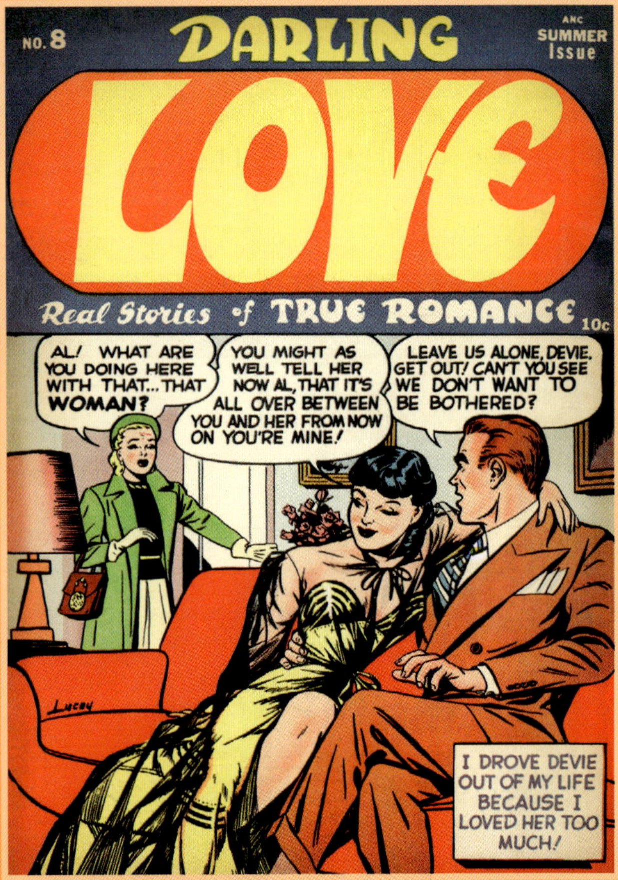

NO. 8
DARLING
ANC
SUMMER Issue
LOVE
Real Stories of TRUE ROMANCE
10c
AL! WHAT ARE YOU DOING HERE WITH THAT... THAT WOMAN?
YOU MIGHT AS WELL TELL HER NOW AL, THAT IT'S ALL OVER BETWEEN YOU AND HER FROM NOW ON YOU'RE MINE!
LEAVE US ALONE, DEVIE. GET OUT! CAN'T YOU SEE WE DON'T WANT TO BE BOTHERED?
I DROVE DEVIE OUT OF MY LIFE BECAUSE I LOVED HER TOO MUCH!

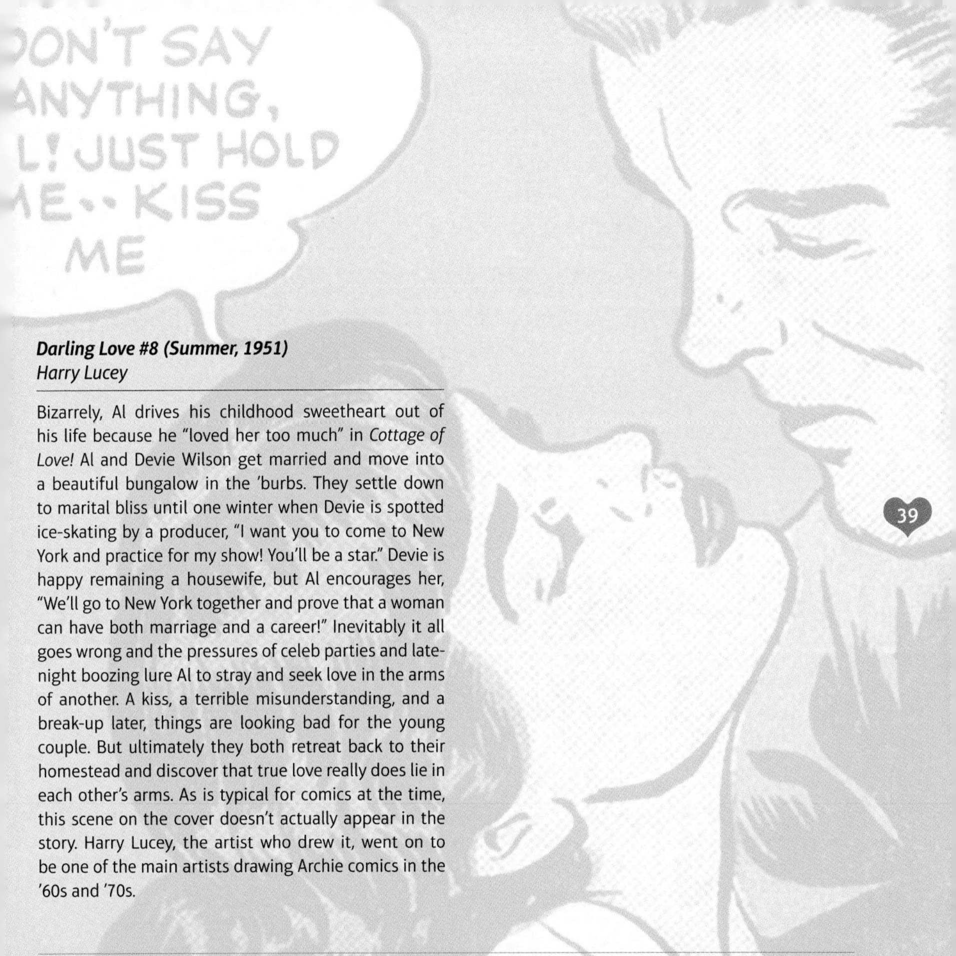
ON'T SAY
ANYTHING,
L! JUST HOLD
E•• KISS
ME

Darling Love #8 (Summer, 1951)
Harry Lucey

Bizarrely, Al drives his childhood sweetheart out of his life because he "loved her too much" in *Cottage of Love!* Al and Devie Wilson get married and move into a beautiful bungalow in the 'burbs. They settle down to marital bliss until one winter when Devie is spotted ice-skating by a producer, "I want you to come to New York and practice for my show! You'll be a star." Devie is happy remaining a housewife, but Al encourages her, "We'll go to New York together and prove that a woman can have both marriage and a career!" Inevitably it all goes wrong and the pressures of celeb parties and late-night boozing lure Al to stray and seek love in the arms of another. A kiss, a terrible misunderstanding, and a break-up later, things are looking bad for the young couple. But ultimately they both retreat back to their homestead and discover that true love really does lie in each other's arms. As is typical for comics at the time, this scene on the cover doesn't actually appear in the story. Harry Lucey, the artist who drew it, went on to be one of the main artists drawing Archie comics in the '60s and '70s.

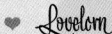

Lovelorn #2 (October-November, 1949)
Artist unknown

Published by American Comics Group, *Lovelorn* had some of the better and more outrageous covers, such as the female lumberjack discovering her beau getting it on with another woman in the woods and her startling self-realization that "... He must think I'm too much of tomboy—I'm not feminine enough for him! I-I thought I loved him—but now I know I hate him!" Good thing she's dropping the axe then! The cover shown here is no exception to this wonderful canon. With the classically stereotyped beret-wearing Frenchman callously declaring, "What do you Americans know about love? We French are born to it!"—warning of the dangers of the Lure of Latin Love. The magnificently xenophobic tale has aspiring American actress Laura dump her agricultural scientist boyfriend, Tom, to study at the Sorbonne in Paris. When Andre the cad steals her heart, puts her in his hit play, and proposes to her, things couldn't go better. But when Andre dumps her for his old girlfriend, Laura is heartbroken. Cue Tom's arrival in Paris, a quick fist-fight, and a theater burning to the ground, and Laura realizes that true love lies in the arms of an all-American boy. Amen!

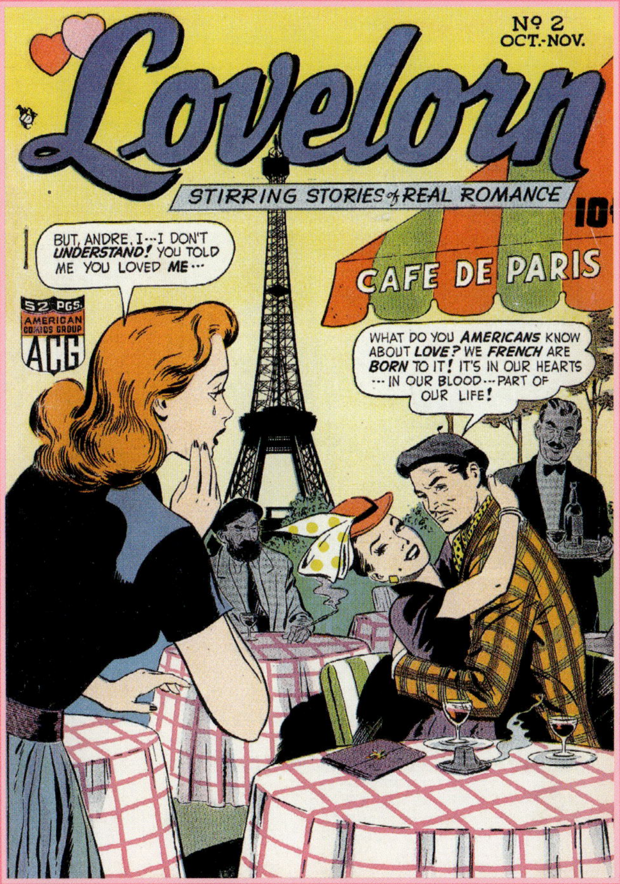
Nº 2
OCT.-NOV.
Lovelorn
STIRRING STORIES of REAL ROMANCE
10¢
52 PGS.
AMERICAN COMICS GROUP
ACG
BUT, ANDRE, I---I DON'T UNDERSTAND! YOU TOLD ME YOU LOVED ME---
CAFE DE PARIS
WHAT DO YOU AMERICANS KNOW ABOUT LOVE? WE FRENCH ARE BORN TO IT! IT'S IN OUR HEARTS --- IN OUR BLOOD --- PART OF OUR LIFE!

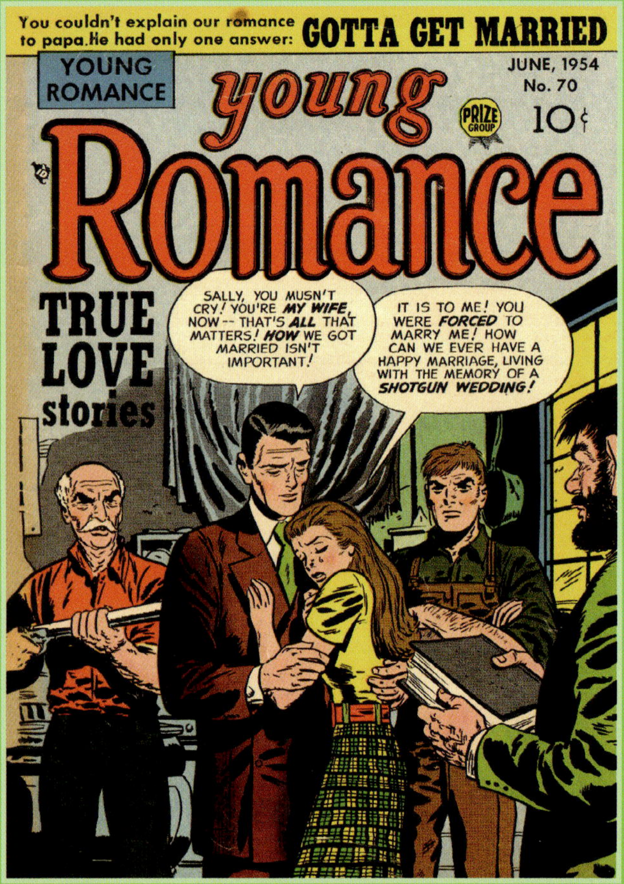
You couldn't explain our romance to papa. He had only one answer: GOTTA GET MARRIED
YOUNG ROMANCE
JUNE, 1954
No. 70
PRIZE GROUP
10¢
young Romance
TRUE LOVE stories
SALLY, YOU MUSN'T CRY! YOU'RE MY WIFE, NOW -- THAT'S ALL THAT MATTERS! HOW WE GOT MARRIED ISN'T IMPORTANT!
IT IS TO ME! YOU WERE FORCED TO MARRY ME! HOW CAN WE EVER HAVE A HAPPY MARRIAGE, LIVING WITH THE MEMORY OF A SHOTGUN WEDDING!

Young Romance #70 (June, 1954)
Bill Draut

Bill Draut was a long-term regular artist illustrating *Young Romance*, working at the Crestwood studio of Jack Kirby and Joe Simon. Draut was 33 when he drew this cover—his only one for *Young Romance*—although technically it is a photostat of the first splash panel of the six-page inside story, *We Gotta Get Married*—also penciled and inked by Draut. "City slicker" Paul falls for country gal Sally. But when Sal's Pa catches them in a midnight tryst he declares, "You little trollop! You'd think nothing of shaming your Pa by sneaking away to make love to a pasty-faced city dude" and demands a shotgun wedding, "a sordid, meaningless ceremony..." Naturally, the course of true love never runs smooth—particularly in comic books—and despite their love for each other, Paul and Sally's marriage is a rocky one. After feeling like an "Ignorant little bumpkin" in the city, she escapes back to her Pa's mountain farmstead. Paul follows and proves his love to Sally by shifting haystacks and beating his love rival half to death. Finally, after the two are reunited, they return to the city with Sally realizing—despite her fears—that, "The sun was shining—because I was with the man who loved me—From now on I'll have the courage to accept that love—anywhere and on any terms."

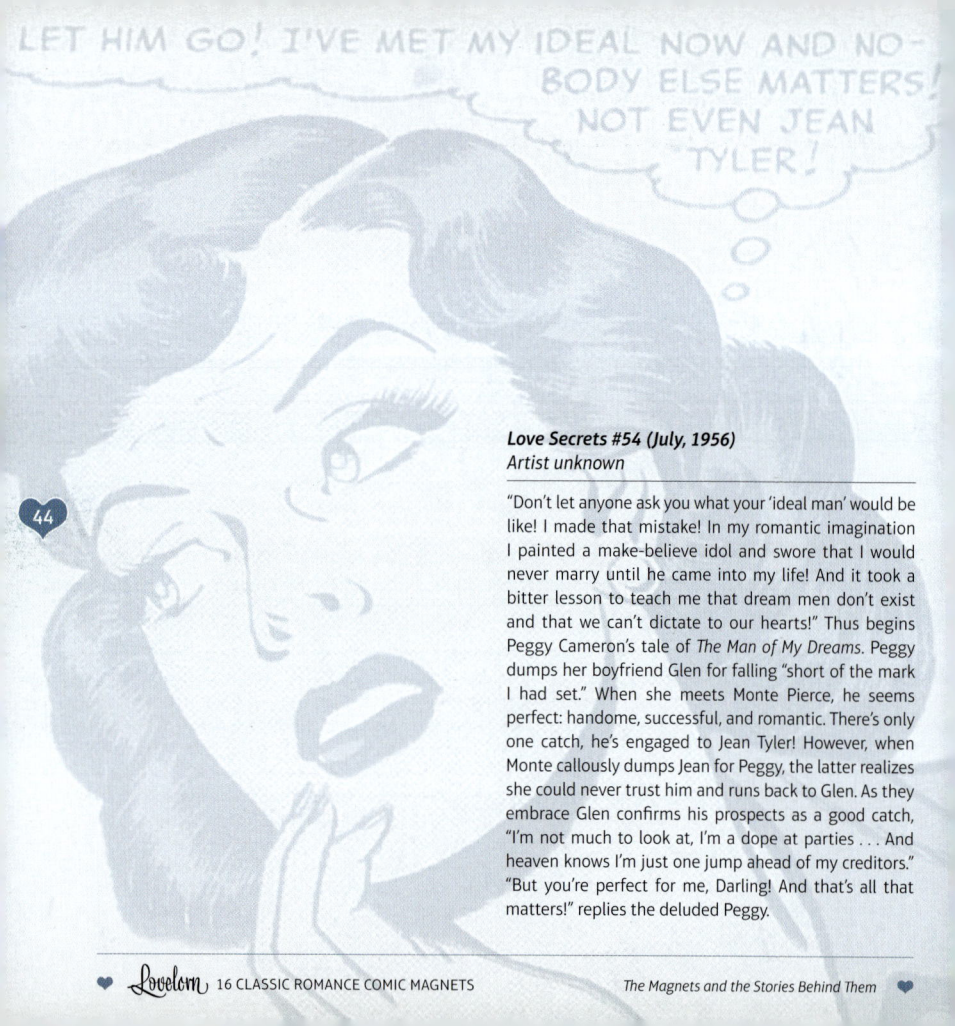

LET HIM GO! I'VE MET MY IDEAL NOW AND NOBODY ELSE MATTERS! NOT EVEN JEAN TYLER!

Love Secrets #54 (July, 1956)
Artist unknown

"Don't let anyone ask you what your 'ideal man' would be like! I made that mistake! In my romantic imagination I painted a make-believe idol and swore that I would never marry until he came into my life! And it took a bitter lesson to teach me that dream men don't exist and that we can't dictate to our hearts!" Thus begins Peggy Cameron's tale of *The Man of My Dreams*. Peggy dumps her boyfriend Glen for falling "short of the mark I had set." When she meets Monte Pierce, he seems perfect: handome, successful, and romantic. There's only one catch, he's engaged to Jean Tyler! However, when Monte callously dumps Jean for Peggy, the latter realizes she could never trust him and runs back to Glen. As they embrace Glen confirms his prospects as a good catch, "I'm not much to look at, I'm a dope at parties . . . And heaven knows I'm just one jump ahead of my creditors." "But you're perfect for me, Darling! And that's all that matters!" replies the deluded Peggy.

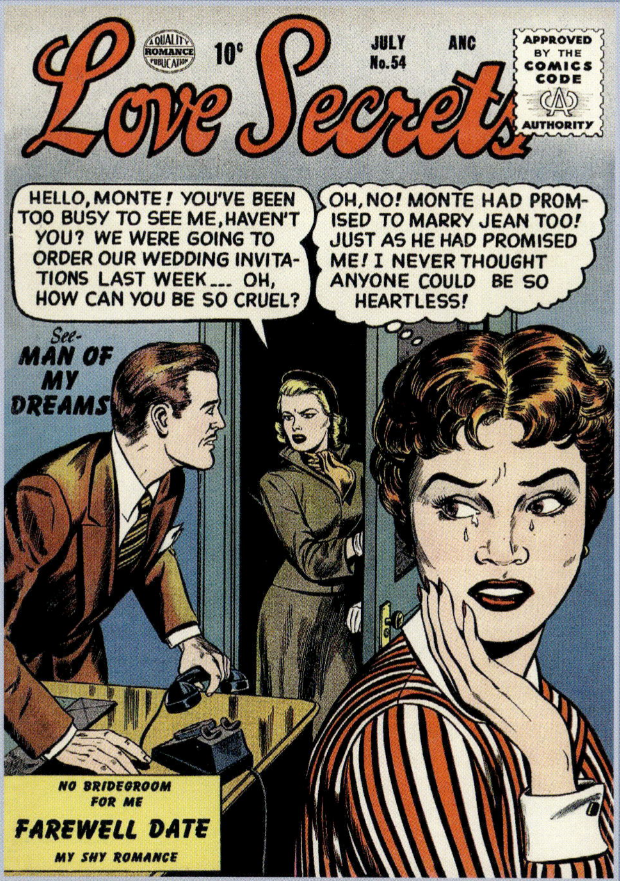
Love Secrets
QUALITY ROMANCE PUBLICATION
10¢
JULY No.54
ANC
APPROVED BY THE COMICS CODE AUTHORITY
HELLO, MONTE! YOU'VE BEEN TOO BUSY TO SEE ME, HAVEN'T YOU? WE WERE GOING TO ORDER OUR WEDDING INVITATIONS LAST WEEK... OH, HOW CAN YOU BE SO CRUEL?
OH, NO! MONTE HAD PROMISED TO MARRY JEAN TOO! JUST AS HE HAD PROMISED ME! I NEVER THOUGHT ANYONE COULD BE SO HEARTLESS!
See- MAN OF MY DREAMS
NO BRIDEGROOM FOR ME
FAREWELL DATE
MY SHY ROMANCE

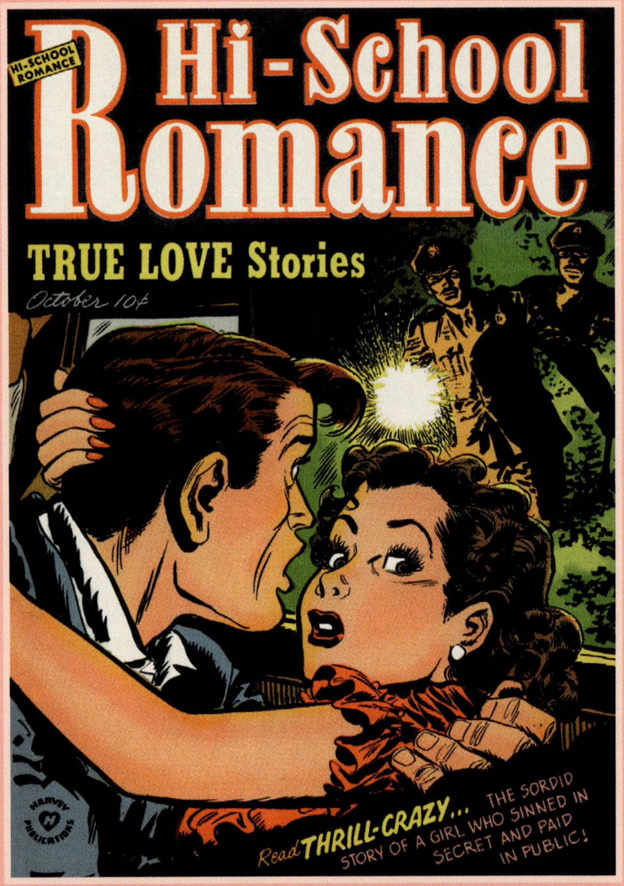
HI-SCHOOL ROMANCE
Hi-School Romance
TRUE LOVE Stories
October 10¢
HARVEY PUBLICATIONS
Read THRILL-CRAZY... THE SORDID STORY OF A GIRL WHO SINNED IN SECRET AND PAID IN PUBLIC!

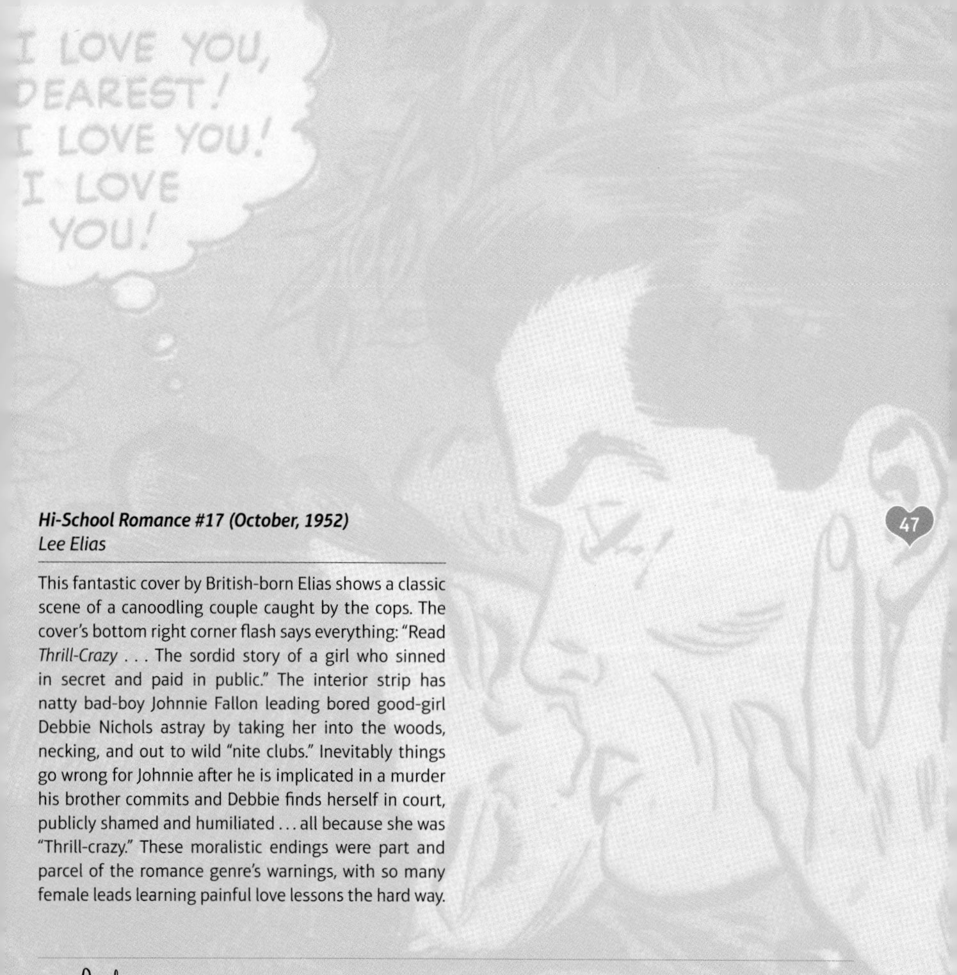
I LOVE YOU, DEAREST! I LOVE YOU! I LOVE YOU!

***Hi-School Romance* #17 (October, 1952)**
Lee Elias

This fantastic cover by British-born Elias shows a classic scene of a canoodling couple caught by the cops. The cover's bottom right corner flash says everything: "Read *Thrill-Crazy* . . . The sordid story of a girl who sinned in secret and paid in public." The interior strip has natty bad-boy Johnnie Fallon leading bored good-girl Debbie Nichols astray by taking her into the woods, necking, and out to wild "nite clubs." Inevitably things go wrong for Johnnie after he is implicated in a murder his brother commits and Debbie finds herself in court, publicly shamed and humiliated . . . all because she was "Thrill-crazy." These moralistic endings were part and parcel of the romance genre's warnings, with so many female leads learning painful love lessons the hard way.

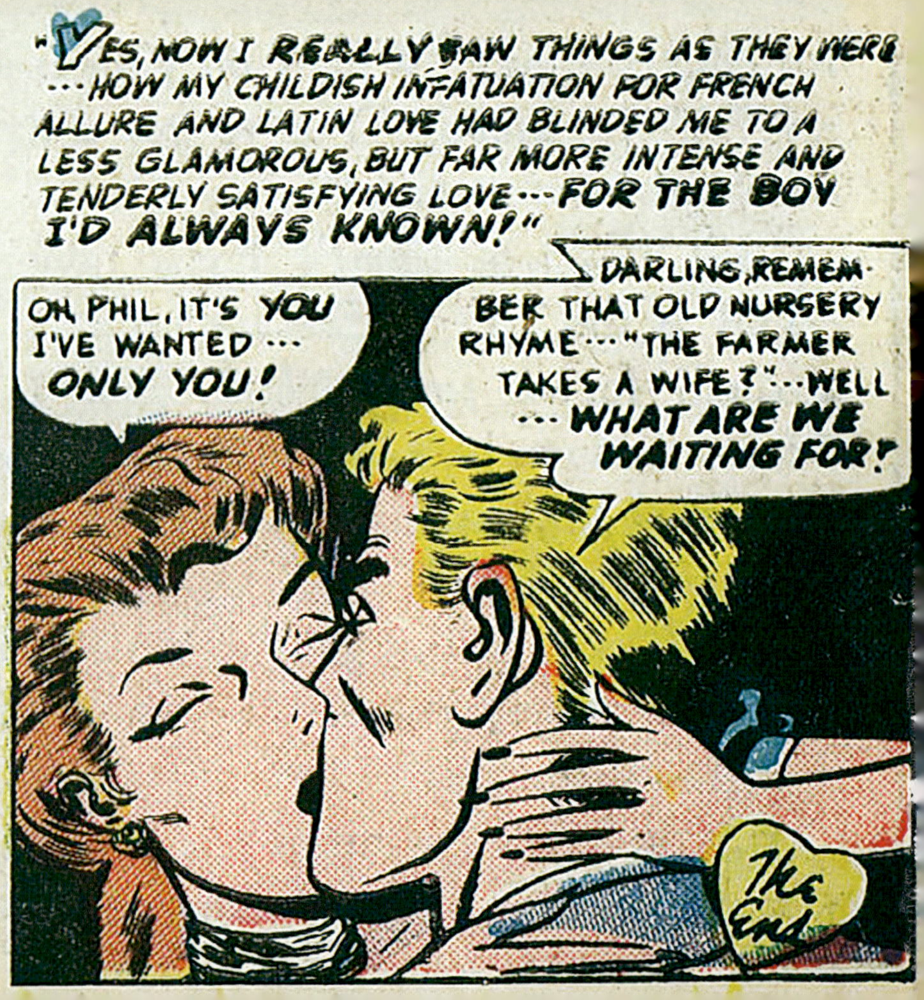
"YES, NOW I REALLY SAW THINGS AS THEY WERE ...HOW MY CHILDISH INFATUATION FOR FRENCH ALLURE AND LATIN LOVE HAD BLINDED ME TO A LESS GLAMOROUS, BUT FAR MORE INTENSE AND TENDERLY SATISFYING LOVE...FOR THE BOY I'D ALWAYS KNOWN!"
OH, PHIL, IT'S YOU I'VE WANTED ... ONLY YOU!
DARLING, REMEMBER THAT OLD NURSERY RHYME..."THE FARMER TAKES A WIFE?"...WELL ... WHAT ARE WE WAITING FOR?
The End